First published 1978

Published by William Collins Sons and
Company Limited, Glasgow and
London
© 1978 William Collins Sons and
Company Limited and Flammarion et
Cie

ISBN 0 00 106145 3
Printed and bound in Spain
by Graficromo, S. A. - Córdoba

Michael Chinery

DISCOVERING ANIMALS

illustrated by
Guy Michel

Collins Glasgow and London

Contents

The animal kingdom	8
Introducing the mammals	10
The king of beasts	12
Thick-skinned giants	14
Animals with hoofs	16
Apes and monkeys	18
Chiselling rodents	20
The cat family	22
The dog family	24
The bears	26
The badger tribe	28
Mammals in the sea	30
Mammals in the air	32
Mammals with pouches	34
Introducing the birds	36
Penguins	38
The parrot family	40
Birds of prey	42
Birds of the sea	44
Birds of fresh water	46
Feathered jewels	48
Crocodiles and other reptiles	50

Reptiles with shells	52
Lizards	54
The snakes	56
The amphibians	58
Frogs and toads	60
Introducing the fishes	62
Some fishes of the sea	64
Freshwater fishes	66
The octopus and the squid	68
Snails, slugs, and bivalves	70
Introducing the insects	72
Butterflies and moths	74
Beetles and flies	76
The social insects	78
Spiders and scorpions	80
Crabs and lobsters	82
Starfishes, urchins, and sea anemones	84
The world of worms	86
Nature in miniature	88
The tree of evolution	90
Index	92

The animal kingdom

The largest animal in the world is the blue whale, a truly gigantic creature which can exceed 30 metres in length and 150 tonnes in weight. At the other end of the scale there are animals too small to be seen without a microscope. These tiny creatures are called protozoans, which means 'first animals'.

Between the protozoans and the huge whales there are about a million different kinds of animals. They include jellyfishes, worms, snails, insects, spiders, starfishes, fishes,

Animals are often divided into two main groups called vertebrates and invertebrates. The vertebrates have backbones inside their bodies. Invertebrates, if they have any skeletons at all, have them on the outside of their bodies.

Although it looks like a flower, the sea lily (left) is an animal related to the starfishes. Hydra (centre) is another animal that looks like a plant because it usually remains fixed to one spot. It is a relative of the sea anemones and catches small animals with the aid of its tentacles. The amoeba (right) is one of the microscopic animals belonging to the Protozoa.

frogs, snakes, birds, and mammals. All of these creatures belong to the Animal Kingdom and they all exhibit the basic features of living things. They all move about, although some move much more than others, and they all take in food and grow. They all breathe and get rid of waste products, and they all react to changes in their surroundings. Finally, they can all reproduce themselves. These seven features separate living from non-living things.

The other great division of the living world is the Plant Kingdom. Plants have the same basic features as animals, but they differ in one very important way. With a few exceptions, plants make their own food from water and other simple substances in the soil and the air. No animal can do this, and all animals have to eat ready-made food. This food all comes initially from plants, although an animal may not get its food directly from plants. An owl, for example, eats shrews and other small animals. Shrews eat slugs, worms, and insects, but these all grow fat on plants. So, really, the owl depends on plants for its food.

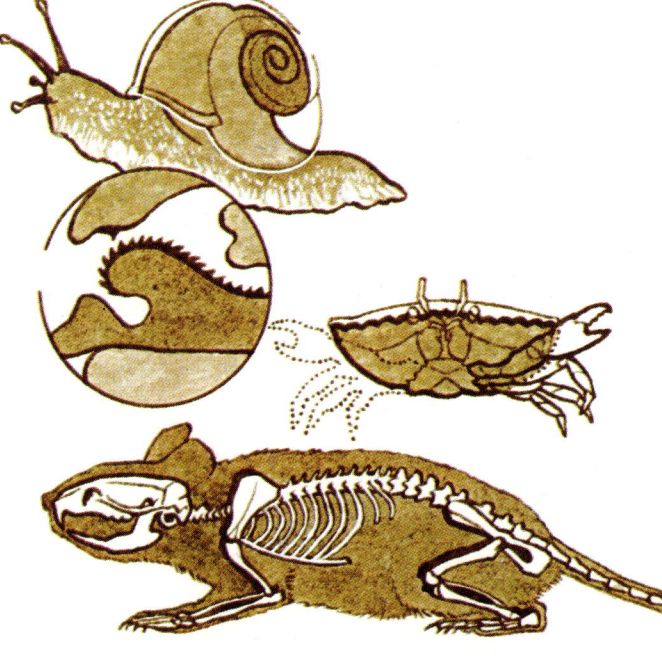

This is a simple example of a food chain or energy chain, but the chain does not really stop at the owl. When the owl dies its body is eaten by beetles and flies, and much of it

way of life. Each has, in effect, carved out a niche for itself in the complex web of life and it has become expert at exploiting this niche to the full. Those kinds or species of animals that failed to establish a suitable niche for themselves became extinct.

The fierce competition for food has meant that every available source is used by some animal or other. Nothing that is edible has been overlooked. Animals that eat flesh are called carnivores, while those that eat plants are called herbivores. Many kinds of animals, including humans, eat both animal and vegetable food and they are called omnivores. Scavengers eat the dung and dead bodies of other animals and play a very important role in keeping the place clean. They also ensure that dead materials are broken down and returned to the soil where plants can use them again. A number of animals, known as parasites, live on or inside the bodies of other animals and steal food from them.

As we shall read later on in this book, all animals have developed or evolved their own clever methods of finding and catching their food. Their teeth and jaws are adapted to their diets, and it is sometimes possible to say what an animal eats just by looking at its teeth.

The giraffe (left) feeds on leaves and is clearly a herbivorous animal, while the secretary bird (below) eats meat and is obviously a carnivore.

decays into simple substances which can be used again by plants.

The land, the sea, the fresh water, and the air have all been conquered by animal life. The hottest deserts have their insects and lizards, while the frozen wastes of the polar regions support seals and penguins. Eleven kilometres down in the sea, sea cucumbers feed on the decaying material that rains down from the waters above. Some insects even manage to live above the snow line on the mountains. They exist on pollen grains and other scraps of debris blown up there by the wind.

Competition for food and living space ensures that only the fittest animals survive. During the millions of years that they have been on the earth each kind has become extremely well adapted to its own particular

Introducing the mammals

Elephants, mice, bats, cats, kangaroos, seals, whales, horses, and people, all belong to the large group of animals which we call mammals. These are generally regarded as the most advanced group of animals, for they have highly developed brains and a much greater ability to learn than other animals. In this respect, man is the most advanced of all the mammals, but in other ways he is not really any different from the other mammals.

The calf above is feeding on his mother's milk – the perfect food for his early life. All mammals feed their young in this way. Young rabbits (below) are naked and helpless when they are born, but their cousins the hares can run about right away. Hares do not live in burrows.

The mammals are all warm-blooded animals, which means that they keep their bodies at a more or less constant temperature. Most of them are clothed with hair or fur which helps them to keep warm. Apart from a few whales, all mammals have at least some hair. Their most important feature, the one that separates them from all other animals, is the fact that the young of mammals are fed with milk from their mothers' bodies.

Mammals have adapted themselves to differing modes of life. Bats fly, whales swim, and moles tunnel in the ground, while many more mammals climb trees or simply run around on the land surface. Their shapes vary enormously according to their ways of life, but they all have the same kind of basic skeleton. Mammals are found almost everywhere, from the steamiest jungles to the freezing polar seas, and they are amazingly adaptable. Polar bears can live quite happily in zoos in warm climates, while lions and zebras from the tropical regions are equally happy in the snow. Such things are possible only because of the mammals' ability to keep their bodies at a constant high temperature.

With the exception of the platypus (see illustration) and its relatives, mammals all give birth to live or active youngsters. Kangaroos and other pouched mammals or marsupials (see page 34) are born at a very early stage and they are then kept in the mother's pouch

The duck-billed platypus of Australia lays eggs in a burrow in the river bank, but like all other mammals, this strange creature suckles its young with milk.

until they are fully developed. The rest of the mammals keep their babies inside their bodies until a much later stage and feed them through a special organ called the placenta. In the placenta, food passes from the mother's bloodstream into that of the baby.

Some gerbils and other mouse-like rodents give birth to as many as twenty babies at a time. Lions and foxes often have four or five cubs in a litter. Twins are common among some monkeys and deer, but most hoofed mammals and the whales normally have only one baby at a time. The nine-banded armadillo is unusual because it always produces quads, and these are always identical in each litter — all males or all females.

Some babies are perfectly formed when they are born and are able to run about within a few minutes. This is very important in animals such as antelopes which are always at the mercy of lions and other carnivores. The young of such animals must be able to keep up with the herd right from the beginning. Young flesh-eating animals with no enemies are usually weak and helpless when they are born and are often naked and blind. Mammals such as rabbits, which are born in the safety of burrows, are also blind and helpless at birth. These young animals are looked after by their mothers for quite a long time, and the fathers may also help with their up-bringing. Flesh-eating animals have a particularly long period of 'childhood', during which they learn how to chase and hunt by playing with their parents and with their brothers and sisters.

Most mammals have some way of defending themselves against their enemies. The armadillo (left) has a suit of armour made of bony plates. Flexible joints allow the animal to roll up. The hedgehog (right) is protected by spines made of very stiff hairs.

11

The king of beasts

An African elephant flaps its huge ears. These large areas of skin act as radiators for the heat generated in such a vast body. The animal's immense weight is carried easily on its pillar-like legs. Surprisingly, the elephant can run fast, although its massive legs do not allow it to jump. The Indian or Asiatic elephant (below right) has smaller ears, and it can also be distinguished by the shape of its back and by the tip of the trunk.

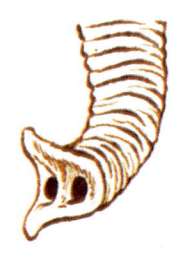

The elephant is the largest and most majestic of all living land animals. Master of all he surveys, he richly deserves his title King of the Beasts. A fully grown African bull elephant stands three and a half metres high and weighs about seven tonnes. His Indian cousin ranges from India to Indonesia, and is slightly smaller. Despite his great size and strength, there is an air of gentleness about the elephant; he can walk or trot amazingly quietly on his huge, pillar-like legs. Travellers in Africa and India tell of waking up in the morning to find elephant footprints all round their tents, and yet they had heard nothing and not even the tent ropes had been disturbed.

An elephant's trunk is formed by the nose and the upper lip. It is very muscular and powerful and has many uses. It is used mainly as a hand to pluck tasty leaves and twigs from the trees, but it can also be used as a shovel to dig up roots, as a drinking straw, as a trumpet, or as a hose to squirt water over itself at bath time. It can also be used to deliver a crushing blow to a troublesome lion or tiger; yet its tip is sensitive enough to pick a small coin out of your pocket.

An animal of such size obviously needs a lot to eat, and a large bull elephant puts away about 400 kilograms of food every day. Leaves, twigs, grass, roots, and bark are its main foods, but the elephant is also very fond of coconuts and other fruits. It shakes the trees until the fruits fall, and then gently cracks the coconuts by treading on them with just the right amount of pressure. If tasty leaves or fruit are just out of reach, the elephant has no hesitation in leaning against the trunk and pushing the whole tree over. The animal also drinks about 200 litres of water every day, sucking up a trunkful at a time and squirting it into its mouth. When water is in short supply the elephants use their tusks to rip open the huge baobab or monkey-bread trees to get at the soft, spongy wood inside.

The elephant's tusks are very large front teeth. They are made of ivory and they go on growing throughout the animal's life: an old male has really massive tusks. Female elephants, which are always smaller than the males, have smaller tusks, and some Indian females have none at all. Tusks are used mainly to defend the youngsters against lions and tigers, but male elephants sometimes fight each other with their tusks.

Apart from their tusks, the elephants have only four teeth in their mouths – one top and one bottom tooth on each side. These teeth are very large and they work like millstones

The immense strength of elephants makes them very useful beasts of burden, especially in hilly and wooded areas where machines cannot go. African elephants can be trained, but they are used less than Indian elephants.

to grind up the food. The teeth gradually wear down and, as the first set wears out, a second set appears behind them. The old teeth fall out and the new ones take over. Six sets of teeth are produced in all, and when the sixth set wears out the elephant starves. It is about 60 years old by this time.

Elephants live in all kinds of country, from dense forest to open grassland and swamps. They live in small herds each of which is ruled by a female. The members of a small herd are nearly all related to each other and help each other. A female who is pregnant gets help from another female who attends closely when the young elephant is born and acts as 'auntie' to it. The females are very good with the youngsters, but the males are less interested and old males often go off to live by themselves. However, the males show great concern when one of their herd is ill or injured, and they always try to help it.

It is commonly said that elephants never forget. We do not know if this is true, but experiments show that the animals certainly have very good memories. They are also very intelligent and can be trained to do various kinds of work as well as to perform circus tricks.

Thick-skinned giants

Next to the elephant, although quite a long way behind it, the largest land animal is the white rhinoceros. This magnificent African beast reaches four metres in length and nearly two metres in height, and it may weigh four tonnes. It is not white at all, and its alternative name of square-lipped rhinoceros is a better one. The animal is a grazer, and it has a very wide, blunt snout which goes over the grass like a lawn mower. White rhinos live in small herds on the savanna, feeding mainly at night and resting during the heat of the day.

The black rhino is somewhat smaller than the white rhino, but it is not any darker in colour. It can be recognized by its pointed and slightly hooked snout. It is a browsing animal and it uses its snout to pull down the branches of trees and bushes. It munches happily on the thorn bushes, quite unaffected by thorns as large as darning needles. Black rhinos usually live alone and they are much more easily startled than white rhinos. They are very short-sighted, probably unable to see anything much more than about fifty metres away, but they have very good hearing and

The hippopotamus (above) generally lives in herds of ten to twenty animals. The animals can actually run along the bed of a river, but they spend most of the daytime floating lazily with just eyes, ears, and nose above the surface. Adult males do not often live with the herds, but spend their time wallowing in muddy pools. The grazing white rhinoceros below shows clearly the wide snout of this species. Notice the oxpecker bird on its back. This bird is a welcome visitor because it removes ticks from the rhino's skin.

All rhinos have thick skin, but the Indian rhino is covered with 'studs' and has great shield-like plates of skin over its shoulders and hips. The animal feeds mainly on tall grasses. The other two Asiatic rhinos – the Sumatran and the Javan – are much smaller creatures and they browse in the dense forests. There are probably only about 100 Javan rhinos left, living in a special nature reserve in Java itself. People in Africa and Asia still believe that to make them feel young again, they should eat ground-up rhinoceros horns. This is untrue, but hundreds of rhinoceroses are killed every year for the purpose, and this is what is making the animals rare.

The hippopotamus

Many people think that the hippopotamus is a relative of the rhinoceros because they are both so big, but they are really very different. The hippopotamus is a very large kind of pig, although its name actually means 'river horse'. It may be four metres long and reach four tonnes in weight. It lives in African lakes and rivers and spends much of the day floating in the water or sunbathing on the bank. Eyes, nose, and ears are all on the top of the head, so that the animal can float with just the top of its head above the surface. The hippo comes out at night to feed on the riverside grasses and other plants. They often eat 200 kilograms of food in a night, using their huge mouths and enormous tusk-like teeth to shovel up the plants. The teeth are also powerful weapons, used against other hippos and against crocodiles, which are their only real enemies. Crocodiles catch young hippos, but an adult hippo can deal easily with the largest crocodile.

an excellent sense of smell. Black rhinos are often said to be bad-tempered animals that charge furiously at anything that disturbs them. They do occasionally charge at cars, but their aggressive reputation is undeserved. Most 'charging' rhinos are simply lumbering up to see what disturbed them.

The three kinds of rhinoceroses that live in Asia are all very rare. The largest is the great Indian rhino, which is almost as big as the white rhino. It has only one horn, however, and can be recognized by its strange armour.

The great Indian rhinoceros shows its armour-like plates of skin very clearly in this picture. It usually lives alone in dense forest or grassland and it enjoys wallowing in mud pools. Like the white rhinoceros, it is a rather placid animal, and usually trots rapidly away when disturbed.

Animals with hoofs

Most of the world's major grasslands support one or more kinds of hoofed mammals. The hoofs are really very large and very tough toe nails which protect the animals' feet while running on the hard ground. The animals walk and run right on the tips of their toes, with the heel a long way off the ground. This arrangement gives the leg extra length and a longer stride, thus giving the animal extra speed. Speed is their main defence against their enemies.

There are actually two groups of hoofed mammals or ungulates, known as the even-toed and the odd-toed. Even-toed or cloven-hoofed mammals include bison, camels, pigs, giraffes, antelopes, deer, sheep, and goats, as well as our domestic cattle. They have either two or four toes on each foot. The odd-toed ungulates are a much smaller group, containing only the horses, zebras, and asses, together with the rhinos and tapirs. They have either one or three toes on each foot as a rule. Antelopes and many other even-toed ungulates have horns on their heads, while most deer have antlers. A horn has a bony core which grows out from the skull and a horny covering made from the same sort of material as is in the hoofs. Horns are often curved and twisted into elaborate shapes but, except in the American pronghorn antelope, they are never branched. In many species both male and female have horns. They are not normally used as weapons, although a male will often drive off a rival by displaying a particularly fine pair of horns.

Antlers have no horny covering and, except in the reindeer, they are carried only by the males. The antlers fall off each year, but you don't usually find old ones because the deer chew them up when they fall. This helps them to grow a new pair for the next breeding season. Male deer usually fight over the females, and the ones with the largest antlers normally win. They do not hurt each other, but simply wrestle and push against each other with their antlers. Each year's antlers are bigger than those of the year before; so it is usually older deer who win these trials of strength and take the females.

Most hoofed mammals live in herds, gaining extra protection from their large numbers. The largest herds are found in Africa, where

The American bison (above), a massive relative of our domestic cattle, once lived in their millions on the Great Plains. The camel (below) is able to live in very dry regions because it saves water very carefully in its body. Its broad hoofs allow it to walk on loose desert sand. This is the two-humped Bactrian camel. Arabian camels have one hump.

The antelope (left) bounds away from danger, while the zebra gallops, but both methods are very speedy and give the animals a good chance of getting away from prowling lions or leopards.

Two red deer stags (below left) engage in a wrestling match. The winner will take the watching female. The diagrams below show the hoofs of a horse and a cow and the footprints of a deer.

hundreds of antelopes and zebras can be seen wandering across the tree-dotted grassland or savanna. But even these herds are small compared with those of a few centuries ago. Large numbers have been killed to make way for crops and cattle. It really would be better to farm the antelopes, because they make much better use of the grasses than cattle. Lots of different kinds of antelopes can live together because each takes a slightly different food. Some feed on tall grasses, others take short ones, and some prefer to browse bushes and low-growing trees.

Not all hoofed mammals live on the grasslands. Most deer are woodland animals, and many small antelopes live in the forests. They eat leaves and bark as well as grass. A lot of even-toed ungulates, such as goats and yaks, live on rugged mountain slopes. Their thick coats protect them from the cold, while their hoofs are specially designed to give them a good grip on steep and slippery rocks.

Raw grass and leaves are not particularly easy foods to digest, and in their stomachs the grazing and browsing animals have armies of minute plants called bacteria to help them break down the tough cellulose of the plants. Antelopes, deer, cows, and many other cloven-hoofed mammals bring food back into their mouths after it has been swallowed and partly digested. This process, known as chewing the cud, aids the digestion.

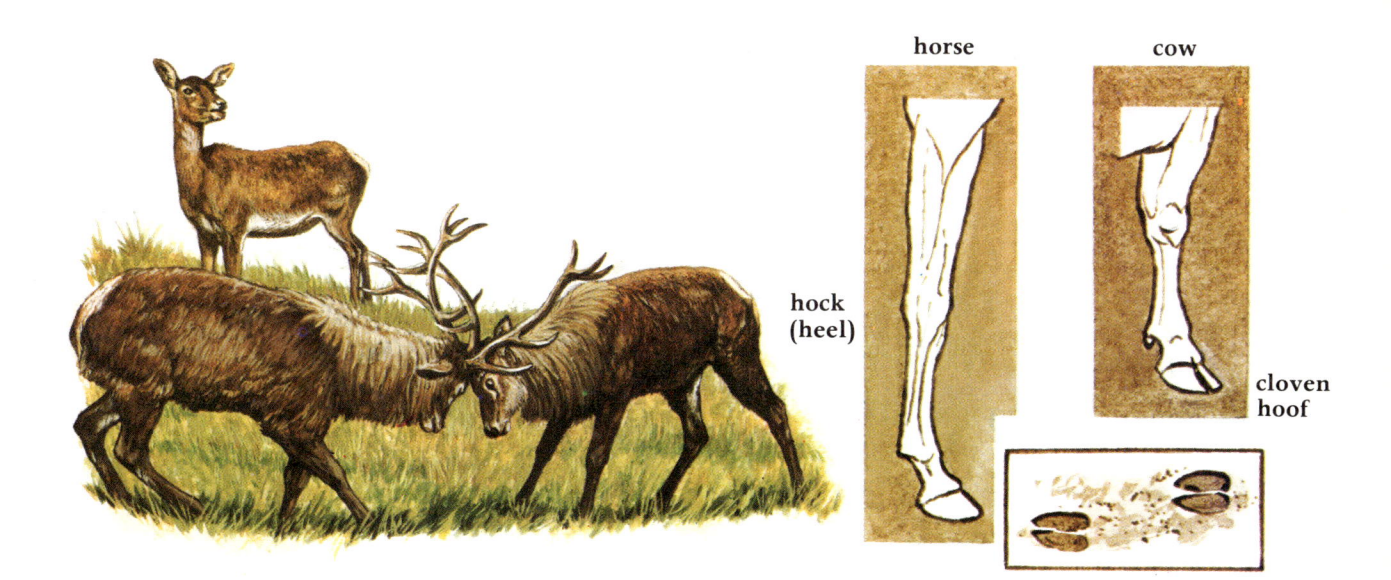

horse

cow

hock (heel)

cloven hoof

Apes and monkeys

The apes and monkeys are our nearest living relatives. If you look at them carefully you will find a lot of similarities between their bodies and ours. The head is usually rounded, with a well developed brain, eyes that look to the front, and ears very like our own. The fingers and toes have nails like ours, and the hands can grasp objects. Apes, monkeys, and men are all included in the group of mammals called primates.

Monkeys have tails, but apes and men do not. It is clear that men are more closely related to apes than to monkeys and that we have descended from some kind of ape, but we did not descend from anything like today's apes. Small apes living perhaps some twenty million years ago split into two groups. One group started to live on the ground and eventually evolved into men, while the other group stayed in the trees and produced today's apes. So, although the apes are our nearest living relatives, they are only very distant cousins.

Apart from the largest males, which sleep on the ground, gorillas build themselves sleeping platforms in the trees every night. Each one chooses a strong branch as a base, bending in slender twigs and branches to form a mattress.

The largest of the living apes is the gorilla. It lives in the African forests and feeds mainly on fruit and leaves. The male may weigh more than 250 kilograms and he is immensely powerful, but he is certainly not the ferocious beast that people once thought. Gorillas live in clans, usually with between ten and twenty animals, each ruled by a mature male. He is the complete master but a kindly one, and he does not usually mind the youngsters playing round him. Many aspects of gorilla behaviour are very much like our own. The chest-beating is rather like an angry man thumping the table: it might frighten another gorilla but it would not normally lead to a fight.

The only other African ape is the chimpanzee. Although much smaller than the gorilla, it is more intelligent and more closely related to man. Chimpanzees spend much more time in the trees than gorillas and feed mainly on fruit. They are agile and extremely noisy

To swing through the trees the orang-utan and other apes and monkeys need good eyesight to judge distances and a good brain to control the movements of the hands and feet.

animals, living in groups with up to 100 animals. There is no true leader as is in the gorilla clan, but the noisiest males tend to dominate. Chimpanzees always sleep in trees. Each night they bend and weave slender twigs among branches as high as 25 metres above the ground to make a bed.

The rest of the apes – the orang-utan and several kinds of gibbons – all live in south east Asia, where they spend almost all of their time in the trees. The gibbons are the smallest of the apes, no more than one metre high, but they have incredibly long arms. They use these to swing hand over hand through the branches and to make huge leaps from tree to tree. Gibbons live in small family groups and warn other families to keep away by making loud hooting noises.

The orang-utan, whose name means 'man of the woods', also has extremely long arms and although not as agile as the gibbons it is a marvellous climber. Its feet can grip just as well as its hands and it can hang effortlessly with any of its four limbs. Like the gibbons, it eats fruit and leaves, together with occasional insects and birds' eggs.

Monkeys are found all over the tropical regions apart from Australia. The baboons of Africa are the largest of the monkeys and live mainly on the ground, but nearly all other monkeys live in the trees. Some of the South American monkeys use their tails to grip the branches and some can even hang by their tails. The tip of the tail has a bare patch just like a finger tip, so it can be used like an extra hand. None of the monkeys of Africa and Asia has this prehensile tail.

Most monkeys feed on the fruit and insects they collect as they scamper through the tree tops. Their intelligence is such that naturalists studying the trees of the tropical jungles have been able to train the animals to go up and collect the flowers and fruits of the trees. Langurs and colobus monkeys feed almost entirely on leaves and, like the hoofed mammals, they have special stomachs to deal with them. Baboons often raid farm land and carry off large amounts of fruit and grain in their large cheek pouches. They also eat small animals and are clever at catching scorpions and nipping off the stings before eating them.

The chimpanzee is the most intelligent of the apes and it actually uses tools. It will use a twig to get insects out from narrow cracks, and it will also use a bunch of leaves as a sponge to soak up drinking water. The mandrill (top) is one of the largest African monkeys, but no naturalist has really explained why it has such a brightly coloured face. Notice the narrow, downward-pointing nostrils typical of the Old World monkeys. American monkeys, such as the woolly monkey (below), have broad, outward-pointing nostrils.

Chiselling rodents

Rats, mice, and their relatives, have four extremely sharp teeth at the front of their mouths. These teeth are just like chisels and the animals use them to gnaw at their food. They can also gnaw their way through a lot of other materials – such as lead pipes and electric cables – in their search for food. The front surface of each tooth is covered by hard,

The tree squirrel (above) is using its sharp teeth to split a nut cleanly in half. The black rat (below) originally came from Central Asia, but it is now a pest in nearly every part of the world.

orange enamel. The rest of the tooth is softer and wears away more quickly, leaving the enamel to form a sharp blade at the tip of each tooth. The blades are kept sharp because, when in use, the top and bottom teeth are always sliding against one another.

These gnawing animals belong to a very large group of mammals called rodents, a name derived from a Latin word meaning 'to gnaw'. With more than 2,000 species they are a very successful group of animals, which are found all over the world. As well as the rats and mice, the rodents include squirrels, porcupines, guinea pigs, beavers, and gerbils. The largest rodent is the South American capybara, which is the size of a pig. Most rodents are much smaller than this, which is one of the reasons why they have been so successful. Individual animals require relatively little food, so a given area can support large numbers. Populations build up quickly because rodents breed so rapidly. For example, a female house mouse living in a grain store may produce ten litters in a year, and each litter may contain five or six young. The young mice themselves start to breed when only about six weeks old.

Rodents are adaptable animals and their rapid breeding means that they can adapt themselves to new conditions much more quickly than other animals. None of them lives in the sea, but rodents are found in every other habitat from the deserts and the tropical forests to the edges of the Arctic Ocean. Some of them even live in towns and in houses, where they compete with us and become pests. The most serious of these pests are the house mouse, the black rat, and the brown rat. Rats and mice are basically seed-eating animals and they do a lot of damage to stored grain, but they have also learned how to deal with many of the other foods that man uses. They are intelligent animals and once established are difficult to get rid of.

The house mouse originally came from somewhere east of the Mediterranean, where it soon latched on to early human civilizations. It has now followed man to all parts of the world, living in houses, ships, and granaries. It is particularly numerous on farms, but the most surprising places which the mice have colonized are refrigerated meat stores. The mice have taken happily to eating frozen meat and they often eat out nesting holes in the carcases. Living in sub-zero temperatures does not seem to bother the animals: they have evolved longer coats to keep themselves warm and they actually grow larger than mice living in warmer places.

Lemmings are small, blunt-snouted rodents with short legs and very short tails. They live in the far north, and the Norwegian lemming is famous for its periodic 'suicide runs' during which millions of animals drown in rivers and the sea. The animals eat grasses and other low-growing plants and every few years their numbers build up so much that there is not enough food to go round. When this happens, the animals seem to panic and they stream out in all directions. They are not trying to commit suicide, for all they want to do is to find somewhere else to live, but they nearly all die on the journey. Those that are left in their original homes have plenty of food and they start to multiply again.

The most famous of all rodents is probably the beaver, who is well known for his building ability. Using his sharp teeth, a beaver takes only a few minutes to fell a tree 15 cm in diameter, and he needs only a few more minutes to gnaw the trunk into short logs. These logs are then dragged or floated down to be added to the beaver's lodge or to the dam which maintains the water level in the lodge pool. The dam is made of logs, branches, stones, and mud, and is sturdy enough for a man or even a horse to walk across the top without causing any damage.

capybara

coypu

jerboa

porcupine

Below: A family of beavers at work on their dam and home (lodge). All the entrances to the lodge are under water.

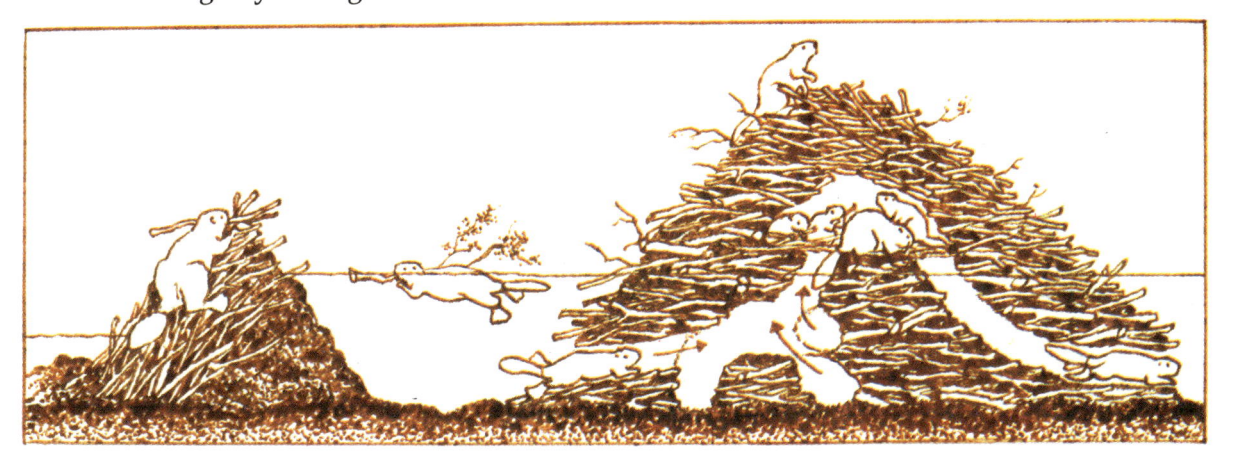

The cheetah can be distinguished from the leopard by the black line running from eye to mouth. The caracal (below) is a very agile grassland cat which can pluck birds from the air as it leaps.

The cat family

The thirty five different kinds of cats are among the world's most efficient hunting animals. All are famous for their stealth and agility, and most have a good turn of speed as well. Compared with the dogs, most cats have rather short, rounded faces. Their jaws also have fewer teeth, but the teeth that they do have are large and sharp and well suited for tearing and cutting flesh. Cats are found all over the world except for the Australian region.

The tiger, lion, leopard, snow leopard, and jaguar are known as the great cats. They are the only ones that can really roar. The other

The bushy black mane of the male lion distinguishes it from all other cats. Each pride usually has only one or two adult males. The animals spend much of the daytime resting under the trees.

cats are known as lesser cats, although the American puma is often larger than the leopard.

The lion is the only cat that lives in large groups. These groups are called prides and each may contain up to about thirty lions. The animals hunt by day or night and, like most cats, rely on their eyes and ears rather than their noses. They prey mainly on the zebra and the gnu, or wildebeeste. The lionesses do most of the hunting, although some always stay behind to look after the youngsters. Working together, the lionesses stalk quietly after their prey, often completely surrounding it before moving in for the kill.

The leopard lives in Africa and Asia, and is a solitary creature, preferring the dense bush and forest. It hunts like our domestic cat, stalking slowly up on its prey and then pouncing when within range. The leopard is the smallest of the great cats, but it is immensely strong and can carry a dead antelope high into a tree to prevent other animals from eating it.

The largest of the great cats is the tiger, which is found in Asia. There are several races of tiger and the largest is the Siberian which has a long, shaggy and rather pale coat. Tigers living in the forests of Malaya are much smaller and darker. The animals like water and usually live near large rivers. Like the leopard, tigers are solitary creatures and they prefer dense cover. Deer and buffalo are their main victims, but they will eat any animal they can catch. Some old or maimed tigers become man-eaters, but the animals usually avoid human settlements, and they do not normally climb trees.

Fastest of all the cats, indeed fastest of all the mammals, is the cheetah. Looking rather like a slender and long-legged leopard, the cheetah can run at speeds of 110 km/h for short distances. Whereas most cats creep up on their prey and then pounce, the cheetah uses its amazing speed to chase after antelopes. It soon gets tired, however, and gives up the chase if it does not make a catch within about 400 metres. Its claws cannot be drawn back into its paw, thus giving it good grip on the ground.

The tiger is very well camouflaged by its stripes as it wanders through the dense riverside reeds.

The largest of the lesser cats is the puma, or mountain lion, which is found throughout North and South America. It looks rather like a small, dark lioness. It is amazingly athletic and can do a high jump of more than four metres. Coming down, it can leap twenty metres without hurting itself. Other well known lesser cats include the lynx, the European wildcat, the ocelot, and the serval. Many have beautifully spotted coats. The domestic cat was almost certainly produced from an African species called the caffer cat.

The ocelot from the forests of tropical America is one of the most attractive cats, but its beautiful skin makes it a target for hunters.

The dog family

African hunting dogs (above) are all very friendly to each other, often bowing and wagging their tails to other members of the pack.

Like the cats, the dogs and their relatives are professional hunters, but the two groups go about their work in different ways. Whereas cats normally stalk their prey, dogs rely on speed and stamina and chase their victims. Most dogs have relatively long legs, which give them longer strides and extra speed. Much more than the cat family, dogs use their noses when hunting, and of course their eyes and ears.

The largest member of the dog family is the wolf, which may be one metre high at the shoulder and 75 kilograms in weight. Wolves once roamed all over the northern hemisphere, but they have been killed off in most places and are now found only in the wilder regions, especially in the far north. Wolves normally mate for life and live in small family groups or packs. Each pack is ruled by the mother and father and it may contain perhaps ten offspring, together with a few uncles and aunts. The adults usually go out to hunt each day in pairs or small groups. They have large appetites, but they always bring back food for those left behind to look after the cubs. Hares, rodents, and small deer provide the wolves with most of their food, but a large pack will work cleverly together to chase and kill a reindeer or even a moose. Their great stamina enables the wolves to run for hours on end, even through deep snow.

The coyote or prairie wolf is a similar, but smaller animal living on the plains of North America. It eats rabbits and other small animals and, like the fox, often enters towns to scavenge from rubbish bins. In Africa and southern Asia the jackal takes the place of the wolf. It is generally smaller than the coyote, but has similar eating habits. Jackals are active at night and often travel in large packs emitting loud, eerie howls. Jackals eat all kinds of small animals, and a pair will often combine to catch a small antelope, but much of their food consists of the scraps left behind by lions and other large hunters.

African hunting dogs live in very well organized societies, usually with twenty or thirty dogs in each pack. A pack hunts over

The sheepdog is one of many domestic breeds. We do not know whether domestic dogs came from wolves or some other kind of dog.

a very wide area, but normally has a base camp somewhere – there the pups are born and looked after. Hunting parties leave the camp just before daybreak to the tune of much barking and howling, which seems to unite the hunters and get them all in the right mood. They stay out for an hour or two, during which time they chase a variety of antelopes. When they see a herd the dogs walk slowly towards it at first: they do not break into a run until the antelopes start to run. The dogs then give chase and gradually single out one antelope for attack, closing in to bite at the victim's legs. As soon as it falls it is killed. The older dogs seem aware that the younger ones must learn to hunt and kill; they always stand back to give the younger ones some practice at bringing down the prey. The young dogs are also allowed to feed first, but then the adults move in and grab large pieces of meat which they take back to camp for the young and their baby-sitters.

The red fox is found almost everywhere in the northern hemisphere. It eats rats, mice and other small animals, including rabbits and birds, and it often goes into towns to find its dinner. The fox is a cunning animal and it is said to 'hypnotise' rabbits sometimes by leaping about frantically and chasing its tail. It gradually moves nearer to its prey and then makes a sudden pounce. Several other kinds of foxes live in various parts of the world. The Arctic fox of the far north turns white in winter to match the snow and it has very tiny ears which do not lose much heat. On the other hand, the tiny fennec fox which lives in the Sahara desert has huge ears. These act as radiators and they also pick up the sounds of small animals moving in the desert at night.

Young foxes (above) play together a great deal. This helps them to learn how to hunt and pounce. The maned wolf (below), which has been described as a fox on stilts, is one of the South American dogs.

The true wolf (bottom) is much more heavily built. Its colour ranges from white (usually in Arctic regions) to black, but it is usually brownish grey.

The bears

Bears are heavily built animals that belong to the same major group as the cats and dogs. They look very cuddly, especially when they are young, but they can be dangerous animals because of their great strength and unpredictable behaviour.

The largest and most dangerous of the bears is the polar bear, which roams the seas and coastlines of the Arctic. It keeps warm by means of a very thick coat and a thick layer of fat under its skin. The polar bear is often seen more than 300 km from land – it travels round the Arctic by hitching lifts on ice floes. It is a tireless walker, trundling over the icy ground without slipping because it has hairy soles on its feet. It swings its head slowly from side to side as it goes and often flicks out its strange purple tongue at the same time. The polar bear feeds mainly on seals and fish and has a very clever way of catching seals when the sea is frozen. It sits by the seals' breathing holes and waits for them to poke their heads up through the water. One slap of the bear's powerful paw kills a seal at once. Polar bears are quite fearless and always come forward to investigate. This is what makes them so dangerous.

Brown bears are found in most of the wilder parts of the northern hemisphere. There are several different races, of which the largest is the Kodiak bear of Alaska. This giant may be nearly three metres long and 750 kg in weight – about the same as the largest polar bear. At the other end of the scale, the Syrian brown bear weighs only about 70 kg. The most famous of the brown bears is the grizzly bear of the Rocky Mountains. This is often said to

The grizzly bear enjoys a fish dinner and frequently paddles in streams to flick out a tasty salmon with a paw.

The Himalayan black bear (top) can be distinguished from the American black bear by the pale band across its chest. The spectacled bear (above) is the only bear living in South America.

Polar bear cubs are born deep in snow caves in the middle of winter. Like all young of the family, they are very small when born and weigh less than one kilogram. Up to four cubs are born at a time and they stay with their mother until nearly a year old. During the summer they may drift about on the ice floes or wander over the land in search of berries and other plant food.

be a bad-tempered animal, but the reputation is generally undeserved. It rarely attacks people unless injured, or provoked, or has lost its fear of man. It is strong enough to kill a bison with one swipe of its paw, but it normally eats only smaller animals such as mice and insects. It also enjoys fish but, like most bears, it eats a lot of plant material and spends a lot of time gathering berries in the autumn.

Black bears live in several parts of the world, including most wooded regions of North America. The American black bear weighs up to 230 kg and climbs trees. It enjoys sweet foods and regularly attacks bees' nests to get at the stored honey. In the American national parks the bears come up to visitors and beg for food, but the wise visitor always stays in his car in case the bears get too inquisitive. They are not normally aggressive, but can get very excited in their eagerness to snatch food, and can then do a lot of damage.

The Himalayan black bear is even less afraid of people and it is a favourite in zoos, with the keepers as well as with the visitors. It regularly stands up on its hind legs to see what is going on. Two smaller black bears – the sloth bear of India and the Malayan or sun bear – both live in southern Asia. The sloth bear has very weak teeth and it feeds almost entirely on the insects called termites (see page 79).

The giant panda, which lives in the bamboo forests of western China, is a close relative of the bears. It is one of the best-loved of all animals, and yet relatively few people have ever seen one alive because few pandas find their way into zoos. Its cuddly appearance is deceptive, however, for it has powerful teeth and claws which can produce nasty wounds. Very little is known about the panda's habits; it is difficult to study because the animal lives in such wild and inaccessible places.

The giant panda's staple diet is bamboo stems, but it varies this with other plants. It also catches birds, small mammals, and fish.

The badger tribe

A family of badgers emerging from their set in the evening. Their living quarters may be a few metres under the ground and furnished with soft grass.

The animals on this page are all carnivores with short legs. They live in a wide variety of ways, but they all belong to a single family known as the Mustelidae. Despite their short legs, most of them are lithe and agile animals. They are found mainly in the cooler parts of the world, especially in the northern hemisphere, and several of them have very fine and valuable fur. The mink and the sable are both reared on fur farms to provide skins for making coats.

The European badger is one of the larger members of the family. Its stout body is about a metre long, but it ambles along surprisingly fast on its short legs. It lives in the woodlands and normally comes out to feed only at night. It catches mice and voles, but most of its food consists of slugs, worms, and insects. The animal also enjoys blackberries and other fruits. All badgers love honey and regularly break open bees' nests to get at it. The honey badger or ratel of Africa is often led to the nests by a little bird called a honey guide. The bird finds a nest and then, by dancing and calling, it attracts the ratel's attention. The ratel follows the bird and then breaks open the bees' nest to get at the honey and the bee grubs. When the ratel has finished, the honey guide moves in to eat the wax combs and any grubs left behind.

Weasels normally live alone, but a female with a family takes her youngsters with her and teaches them to hunt. The animals very often stand up on their back legs and look around them.

The weasels are the smallest members of the family. The common European weasel is only about 22 cm long with an incredibly slender body. It is also a relentless killer. It attacks rabbits and poultry far larger than itself and kills far more than it needs to eat. Its main food consists of mice and voles, which it can follow right down into their tunnels. The stoat is a larger version of the weasel, distinguished by the black tip to its tail. In the winter in the colder regions the stoat's coat turns white and it is then known as an ermine, although the tip of the tail stays black. Stoats feed mainly on rats and rabbits. The ferrets which people sometimes use to catch rats and rabbits are domesticated forms of another relative called the polecat.

The martens are mainly tree-living animals and they are amazingly agile. They chase and catch birds and squirrels in the trees. Most of them have beautiful soft fur which keeps them warm in their northern homes. They are generally rather shy, but the beech marten of Europe does not seem to mind people so much and it sometimes takes up residence in town parks.

Largest of the land-living mustelids is the wolverine, which lives all round the Arctic circle. A metre long and 60 cm high, it looks rather like a small bear, and it has a bear's appetite as well. It is often called the glutton because it eats so much. It will eat any animal it can find, including dead ones, and its great strength enables it to pull down animals as large as reindeer or even moose. But it does not eat them all at once: it buries what is left for another day.

The otters are the water-loving members of the badger family. They live in rivers and marshes, where they eat fishes, frogs, water birds, and many other animals. Some otters also live on the sea shore. They all have sleek, waterproof fur and a stout tail which is used as a rudder. They are wonderful swimmers, able to stay under water for long periods without coming up for air. Otter babies are born in burrows in the river bank and the mother has to force them to go into the water when they are about eight weeks old. Once they have been in, however, they love it and spend hours sliding down the bank and then climbing up for another go.

The sea otter is the largest of all the mustelids, with a weight of up to 36 kilograms. It lives round the coasts of the north Pacific Ocean and normally comes ashore only to have its young. It eats crabs and other shellfish, often floating on its back and cracking the shells open on a stone held on its chest.

The otter is a playful animal and loves to slide in the snow. Its thick coat keeps it warm.

The pine marten lives in the coniferous forests of Europe. It eats berries as well as animal food.

The skunk is an American mustelid famous for its unusual, but very effective defence. It turns round and fires a stinking fluid from glands near the tail, often standing on its front legs to do so.

The Biscayan whale (above) is one of the whalebone whales. You can see the long strips of whalebone hanging like a curtain from the upper jaw. This whale was once common in the North Atlantic, but whalers caught so many that it is now a rare species.

Mammals in the sea

Mammals are basically land-living animals, but three groups – the whales, the seals, and the sea-cows – have taken to life in the sea. The whales are the most highly adapted of these marine mammals and cannot leave the water. The largest animal that ever lived on earth is the great blue whale. Not all whales are particularly big – some dolphins are only about two metres long.

The whale's body is beautifully streamlined for easy movement through the water, with only the two flippers breaking the smooth outline. These flippers, which are used for steering and balancing, look quite different from the front limbs of land-dwelling mammals, but the bones inside are actually quite similar. The hind legs have completely disappeared, and the tail has developed into a powerful paddle which pushes the whale through the water.

Although wonderfully adapted for life in the water, whales still have to come up to breathe. Air is taken in and eventually blown out through a 'blow-hole' on the top of the head. When a whale comes to the surface the spout of stale air is clearly visible because of the water vapour and oily droplets that it contains. The sperm whale can dive for up to two hours without coming up for air, and it can go down to nearly 1000 metres, but most whales surface every five or ten minutes. The animals sleep while floating, with just the blow-hole above the surface.

The females give birth to their young in the water and immediately push them up to the surface to take their first breaths. A young blue whale weighs about two tonnes at birth. When she is actually giving birth and when pushing the baby to the surface, the mother whale may be helped by another female. Co-operation of this kind shows that whales are intelligent animals, and recent studies have shown that they 'talk' to each other with a wide variety of sounds.

There are two very distinct groups of whales – the toothed whales and the whalebone whales. Toothed whales include the dolphins, the

The bottle-nosed dolphin (left) is often kept in zoos and aquaria, where it can be taught to perform several tricks. It is a very intelligent and playful animal which lives in large groups, or schools, out in the ocean.

killer whale, and the sperm whales. They all have numerous pointed teeth well suited to grasping their prey. The smaller whales eat fishes, but the killer whale, which may be 10 metres long, eats other whales, seals, and penguins. The square-headed sperm whale, which may be 20 metres long, feeds mainly on the giant squid (see page 69). The squid puts up quite a fight, and many sperm whales carry scars showing where they have been wounded by the squid's suckers.

Whalebone whales have no teeth and they feed in a very different way. Plates of a horny material called baleen or whalebone hang down from the upper jaws like the teeth of a giant comb, and the whales use these to strain millions of small shrimp-like animals from the surface layers of the sea. It might seem strange that the largest animals in the sea feed on some of the smallest, but this is really very efficient because it cuts out the middle links in the food chains.

Seals and sea lions

Seals spend quite a lot of time out of the water, and always give birth to their young on land. Their bodies are less fully adapted for life in the water than those of the whales, but they are, nevertheless, excellent swimmers. Both front and hind limbs are in the form of flippers, although seals and sea lions use them in different ways. Seals use their front flippers only for steering. The hind flippers are held close together and they trail out behind the body like a tail. By waving them strongly from side to side, the seal pushes itself through the water. Sea lions and their relatives, the fur seals, use their front flippers to paddle themselves through the water and use the trailing hind flippers as a rudder. Both seals and sea lions feed mainly on fishes, although some of the Antarctic seals catch penguins.

In the breeding season the seals and sea lions collect on the beaches, often in enormous numbers. Adult males, particularly among the fur seals and the huge elephant seals, gather groups of females around them and fight off other males. The females give birth to their babies and then mate with their masters before going off to sea again.

Sea lions and fur seals (top) can turn their hind flippers forward and use them to waddle about on land. True seals can only wriggle about on land. The walrus (below) is a large seal living in the Arctic. It uses its tusks to defend itself and also to dig for shellfish in the mud.

The dugong (below) belongs to a small group of mammals called sea cows. It lives in coastal waters and eats plants. Its habit of floating on its back with the front part of the body out of the water gave rise to the legend of the mermaid. Dugongs live only in the Indian and Pacific Oceans.

The 'wings' of the colugo (left) are covered with fur, making the animal, when at rest, look as if it is wrapped in a woolly blanket.

Mammals in the air

Several tree-living mammals move through their forest homes by gliding from tree to tree. Their 'wings' are flaps of skin stretched out along the sides of the body between the front and back legs. A number of different kinds of 'flying squirrels' glide in this way, and so do various Australian phalangers (see page 35), but the champion gliders are the colugos of south east Asia. These animals are about 40 cm long and they are not closely related to any other mammals. They have large flaps of

An insect-eating bat closes in on a moth. When it has been caught in the mouth the moth may be tucked into the flap of skin between the bat's back legs and carried away to be eaten.

skin stretching from the wrist to the ankle on each side, and another one between the two back legs. By altering the position of their 'wings', these animals can cover 400 metres or more in a single glide, but we cannot say that they really fly because they do not flap their wings.

The only mammals that really fly are the bats. The wings of these animals are generally rather thin and they are supported mainly by the enormously long, thin fingers. The wing membrane extends along the sides of the body enclosing the back legs and tail. Because they have no ordinary limbs, the bats are almost helpless on the ground. They rest mainly in trees or on the ceilings of caves and buildings always upside down and gripping with the toes of their hind feet.

The bats can be conveniently divided into two main groups, which we can call small bats and large bats. The small bats, which are mostly the size of mice, feed mainly on insects and their mouths bristle with sharp teeth. They are all active at night, when they catch huge numbers of moths and beetles. Their eyes are weak, but they have developed a wonderful system of radar for finding their way about in the dark. The system is called echo-location.

The whole time that the bat is flying it gives out a stream of high-pitched sounds. These are far too high for us to hear, but the bat's large ears pick up the echoes of the sounds as they bounce back from nearby objects. Even in complete darkness, the bat can work out where these objects are and avoid them when flying at full speed. The same system is used for catching insects. The bat somehow distinguishes between the flying insects and stationary objects and catches the insects in mid air. Most of them are eaten in flight, but larger moths may be carried to a perch to be eaten. Insect-eating bats in the cooler parts of the world, such as Europe, pass the winter in a deep sleep called hibernation. They could not survive otherwise because there are few insects about in the cold weather.

The blood-sucking vampire bat of tropical America is one of the small bats. It is only about seven cm long, but its habits make it a very dangerous animal. It feeds on the blood of birds and mammals, including man, and usually attacks them while they are asleep. Unlike other bats, the vampire is quite agile on the ground and can scuttle about until it finds an exposed part of the body. If often attacks the legs and its teeth are so sharp that the victim does not feel the bite. The bat then simply licks up the blood flowing from the wound. The wound itself is not particularly bad, but the vampire can carry the dreadful disease rabies and this is why it is so dangerous.

Another group of small bats feed on fishes. These fish-eating bats are larger than the insect-eaters and they skim low over coastal waters and rivers in Central America. They use their echo-location system to detect ripples on the surface, and then they swoop down to catch the fish that made the ripples.

The large bats all live in tropical areas and they eat fruit and nectar. They have long snouts, but their teeth are small and weak because of their soft food. Their bodies are up to 30 cm long, and their black wings are as much as 150 cm across. The largest kinds are known as flying foxes because of their rich

A fruit-eating bat bites into a bunch of bananas. These bats do a tremendous amount of damage in fruit plantations. Notice that in this group of bats the skin flap is not fully developed between the back legs.

brown fur and their fox-like faces. The fruit-eating bats use their eyes to find their way about, but they also have a simple form of echo-location. Instead of producing high-pitched sounds, they make clicking noises with their tongues. During the day these bats hang in the trees in such numbers that they often break the branches.

Flying foxes hanging up to rest and stretching their wings in readiness to fly off to feed. Before letting go with its feet the bat flaps its wings to bring its body into a horizontal position.

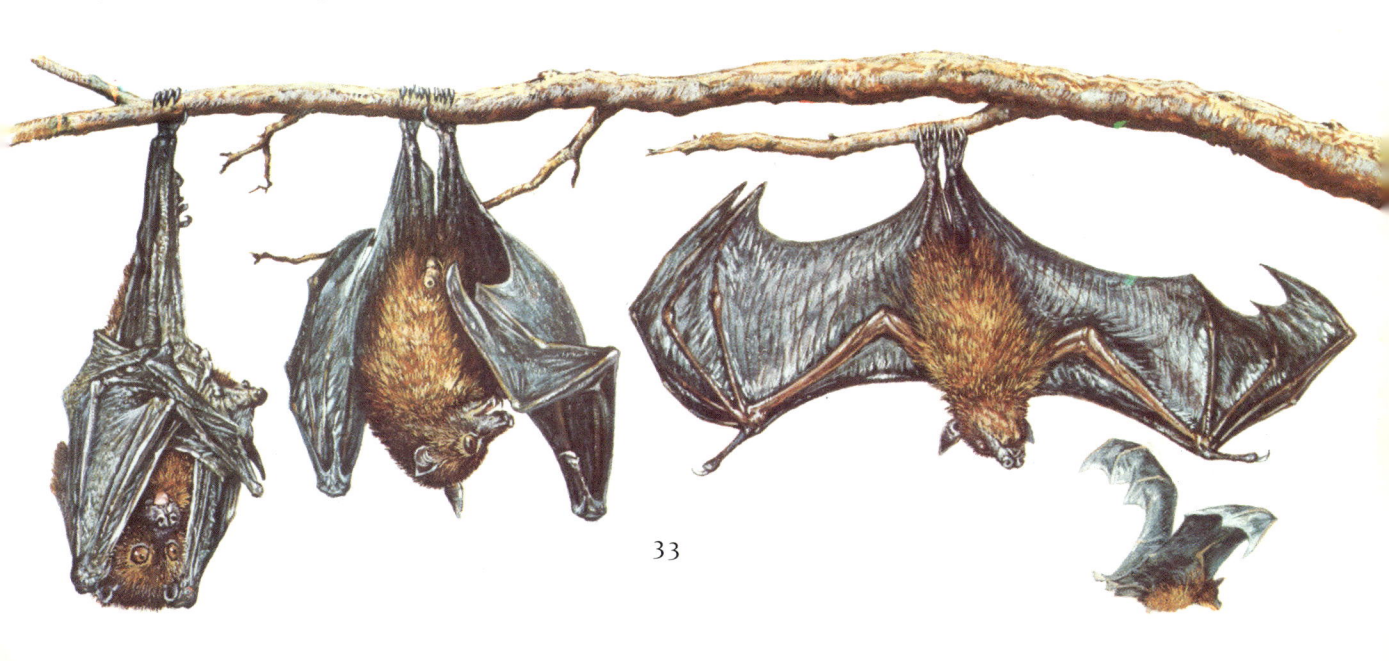

Mammals with pouches

The pouched mammals are almost entirely confined to Australia and neighbouring islands. Their young are born at a very early stage, when they are very tiny and hardly look like young animals at all. They have to spend quite a long time in a pouch on their mother's body before they get their proper features. The mother's milk glands open into her pouch, so the babies have a supply of food on tap at all times. This is a rather primitive way of producing young and the pouched mammals, or marsupials, are not closely related to the other mammals.

There are about 180 different kinds of marsupials alive today. They include kangaroos, wallabies, wombats, opossums, phalangers, bandicoots, and that most lovable of all Australian animals, the koala. Many of these pouched animals are very similar to mammals in other parts of the world because they lead similar lives. There is, for example, a marsupial mole which, in general behaviour and appearance, is remarkably like the moles of the northern hemisphere. The marsupial mole is white or brown, whereas the true moles are black, but this is only a minor detail. This similarity between unrelated animals leading similar lives in different parts of the world is called convergent evolution. The nearly extinct Tasmanian wolf provides another well-known example through its similarity to the timber wolf of northern lands. But however similar these animals appear, their breeding methods remain very different.

The largest of the marsupials are the red kangaroo and the great grey kangaroo, both of which may reach two metres in height. The smaller kangaroos are generally called wallabies, but they all have similar bodies with long back legs and a stout tail which can be used as a support and as a rudder. They are all vegetarians and they are the Australian equivalents of the deer and antelopes in other parts of the world. Their leaping movements are very different from the running of these other mammals, but they serve exactly the same function of carrying the animals rapidly

The grey kangaroo standing up and using its tail as a third leg to support its body. The inset shows the actual size of the newly born kangaroo. It weighs about 30 gm at this time.

The baby koala spends about six months in its mother's pouch, and then a further six months riding on its mother's back. Strong legs and sharp claws give the animals a firm grip on the branches.

over the ground. If you look at the head and jaws of a kangaroo you will see that they are very similar in shape to those of an antelope and clearly adapted for the same kind of food. Like the antelopes, some kinds of kangaroos are grazers, while others prefer to browse on bushes. Some small kangaroos actually live in the trees.

The koala is an attractive bear-like animal which is often called the Australian teddy bear. It lives high in the eucalyptus or gum trees and hardly ever comes down to the ground. Eating nothing but the leaves and shoots of these trees, the animals themselves smell strongly of cough mixture.

Wombats are short, podgy animals that live in long tunnels under the grasslands. They have very strong claws and are sometimes called Australian badgers. Unlike true bad-

The bandicoot's pouch, like that of several other ground-living marsupials, opens to the back. It does not then get full of dirt as the animal moves.

nosed bandicoot is a dainty eater and always cleans its food before eating it.

Phalangers or Australian opossums live in the trees and are the Australian equivalents of monkeys and squirrels. Several have prehensile tails like the American monkeys, while others glide on flaps of skin like flying squirrels (see page 32).

Marsupials once lived all over the world, but they were replaced in most parts by the more advanced mammals. Australia became separated from the other continents before many of these other mammals could reach it, and so the marsupials survived there.

The Virginia opossum of North and South America is one of the few marsupials living outside Australasia. It is an excellent climber, even when several young are riding on its back.

The banded anteater or numbat uses its strong claws to break open termite nests and it then licks up the juicy insects with its long tongue.

gers, they are purely vegetarian and eat nothing but grass and other plants when they come out at night. The rare Tasmanian devil is really much more like a badger in its habits. It lives in the woodlands and comes out to hunt other animals at night.

Bandicoots are long-snouted marsupials ranging up to the size of a rabbit. They feed mainly on insects and earthworms which they find by scratching up the ground with their sharp claws. The animals often annoy gardeners by rooting around among the plants. The long-

Introducing the birds

The birds, like the mammals, are warm-blooded creatures, which means that they keep their bodies at a constant temperature no matter what the surroundings are like. But birds and mammals are built on completely different lines, for the whole body of a bird is built for life in the air. It has a very light skeleton, and its front limbs are wings. The body is covered with feathers which, as well as keeping the bird warm, provide a smooth outline and the broad wing surfaces necessary to keep the bird aloft.

The scales on a bird's leg suggest that, many millions of years ago, birds descended from reptiles, and it seems certain that a bird's feathers are really glorified scales. They were probably concerned only with keeping the bird warm to start with, and became involved with flight later. The birds probably descended from some kind of tree-living reptile which climbed about in the branches and

A swallow feeding its young at the nest. The young birds automatically open their beaks wide when the parent arrives, and she pushes insects in.

great spotted woodpecker

Feathers form the broad wing surface which keeps the bird in the air. Most birds use flapping flight, moving the wings up and down regularly and twisting them at the tips to push the air back and

glided from tree to tree. Gliding performances would have improved as feathers covered the front limbs, and then both wings and feathers grew larger and more efficient.

Although all birds have wings and feathers, quite a few species have given up flying and their wings are generally small and weak. Among these flightless birds are the ostrich, the kiwi, and the now extinct dodo.

Feathers are often very brightly coloured and they play an important part in the courtship displays of the birds. Normally, only the males are brightly coloured and these birds display their lovely feathers to the females. Sounds are also an important feature of courtship, many birds winning a mate by singing beautiful songs at the beginning of the breeding season.

The heads and beaks of birds with different diets. Buzzard, a flesh eater. Pigeon, a mixed feeder. Warbler, an insect eater. Chaffinch, a seed eater. Swallow catches insects in flight. Woodpecker probes tree trunks for insects. Curlew probes mud for food.

chaffinch

buzzard **pigeon** **warbler**

force the whole body forward. Each feather consists of a main stem or shaft with lots of interlocking barbs. If the barbs become separated, the bird preens them into position with its beak.

Like the mammals, the birds have made use of almost every available kind of food. Warblers eat insects, sparrows eat seeds, hawks eat meat, and kingfishers eat fish, and yet none of the birds has any teeth to help it. With no front legs or hands either, the beak has to do almost all the work of catching and cutting up the food, although seed-eating birds have a very muscular gizzard which helps to grind up the seeds.

Just as mammals have different kinds of teeth to deal with different kinds of food, so the birds have many different kinds of beaks, each suited to their particular diets.

Many birds spend one part of the year in one place and the rest of the year somewhere else, perhaps thousands of kilometres away. The swallow, for example, spends the summer in Europe, but flies off in the autumn to spend six months in Africa. It could not find enough insects to eat during the winter in Europe. These long journeys are called migrations and the birds find their way by the sun and the stars. Some even return to the same nest every year.

All birds lay eggs, and most birds build cosy nests for them. Twigs, moss, grass, mud, wool, and even spiders' webs are used in building the nests. Some birds, such as long-tailed tits, make closed, ball-shaped nests, but most nests are cup-shaped and open. Many birds make no more than a shallow hollow in the ground, while some sea birds simply lay their eggs on rocky cliff ledges. One or both parents have to sit on the eggs to keep them warm until they hatch, but ostriches and some other tropical birds have to sit on their eggs to shade them and keep them cool. The mound-builders of Australia incubate their eggs in a very strange way: they bury them in piles of rotting plants and use the heat of fermentation to keep the eggs warm. The European cuckoo and a few other birds avoid the whole business of making nests and incubate their eggs by getting other birds to do it for them. They simply lay their eggs in the other birds' nests and leave them there. The foster parents feed the young cuckoos as if they were their own young.

The ostrich is the world's largest living bird, reaching a height of 2·5 metres. It runs swiftly on its stout legs and has very fluffy feathers. Because it does not fly, it does not need smooth plumage.

swallow woodpecker curlew

Penguins

The penguins are flightless sea birds living in the southern hemisphere. They are popularly regarded as birds of the frozen Antarctic, but only five of the eighteen kinds of penguins actually live inside the Antarctic Circle. The rest live on the numerous sub-antarctic islands and around the coasts of Australia, New Zealand, South Africa, and South America. The Galapagos penguin actually lives very close to the Equator.

All penguins have black backs and white fronts, but there are often coloured patches on the head or beak and several species have coloured plumes on the head. Although flightless, the birds have powerful, oar-like wings which they use to drive themselves along, almost as if they were flying under water. They can move very fast to chase fish or to escape from the seals which eat them. The birds can also swim on the surface of the water, sitting there like rather long ducks and paddling away with their webbed feet. On land, the birds waddle along in an upright position, looking rather like small men in dinner suits, but in icy conditions they will get down on their fronts and slide down slopes like little toboggans.

The penguin's outer feathers are like overlapping scales which are not broken up into barbs like ordinary feathers. They are densely packed and covered with oil to keep the water out. An inner layer of downy feathers and a thick layer of fat under the skin keep out the cold and give the birds a good chance of surviving the iciest conditions.

Penguins living in the warmer parts of their range make their nests in burrows or among the coastal grasses, but those of the true Antarctic have to make other arrangements. The emperor penguin, which is the largest species, breeds on the bare snow and ice, right in the middle of the Antarctic continent's long, dark winter. The birds leave the sea and walk or slide as much as 100 kilometres inland to the breeding sites or rookeries, where they

A penguin 'flying' after fishes in the water. The sharp beak is well suited for grasping slippery fishes. The penguins also eat squid (see page 69) and the little shrimp-like creatures that are so common in the cold Antarctic waters.

Adélie penguins often catapult themselves out of the water by swimming very quickly up to the surface. This is a good way of escaping the seals.

pair up and lay the eggs. Each female lays just one egg and almost immediately passes it over to her mate. The birds must be very careful not to drop the egg, for it would freeze and die as soon as it touched the ice. The male bird places the egg on top of his feet and covers it with a thick fold of skin from his stomach. This is the beginning of a long, patient wait while the female goes off to the sea to feed.

There may be several thousand egg-minding males at a rookery, huddling together to keep warm. They have no food and they stay still to conserve their energy. The eggs are ready to hatch in about two months and, using some very efficient kind of internal clock, the females return just in time to feed the young chicks with fish that they have brought back in their stomachs. The females take over their chicks and the males, who have not eaten for nearly three months, trudge back to the sea to feed. They return to the rookeries after two or three weeks and continue to feed the chicks with regurgitated fish while the females go off again. By this time, however, the ice is breaking up all around the continent and the penguins do not have far to go to the water. Soon, both parents are going off to fish each day, leaving the youngsters standing together in huge nurseries. By grouping together in this way the young penguins protect themselves from attacks by big gull-like birds called skuas. Somehow, the parent penguins find their own chicks again when they return with food. By the time the ice breaks up completely, the young penguins have their waterproof coats and can go off to sea.

The only other penguin that normally breeds on the Antarctic continent is the Adélie penguin, but this species breeds in the Antarctic spring – October or November. The birds mate for life and always use the same nest site.

A young Adélie penguin thrusts its head into its parent's beak to get some fish. Behind, two adult birds greet each other on returning to the nest.

A young emperor penguin peers out from its snug retreat under its parent's body. Its fluffy feathers will soon be covered with thick waterproof ones.

royal penguin   gentoo penguin   king penguin   Galapagos penguin

The parrot family

The parrots and their relatives, which include the cockatoos and the budgerigars, are among the world's best known and best loved birds. Huge numbers are kept as pets, partly because of their bright colours and partly be-because of their fascinating ability to 'talk'. Parrots and budgerigars are great imitators and they soon pick up words used regularly by their owners. It is quite easy to teach a bird to say a few simple sentences, but it does not understand what it is saying: it is merely repeating what it hears. The parrots are, nevertheless, among the most intelligent of birds and quite a number have learned how to undo the locks on their cages and let themselves out. Another reason for their popularity as pets is their long life: several parrots and macaws are known to have lived for more than sixty years.

There are over 300 different kinds of birds in this family, distributed all over the warmer parts of the world. In the forests of Africa and tropical America the birds are largely green in colour, but there are some very colourful species in the Australian region where they have fewer enemies. All members of the family have the familiar hooked beak. This looks rather similar to the beak of flesh-eating birds

The macaw is a large, brightly coloured parrot from South America. Like all parrots, it has two toes pointing forwards and two pointing backwards on each foot. This is ideal for gripping and climbing.

A pair of lovebirds 'kissing'. As in most parrots, the males and females are much alike.

A flock of budgerigars swooping down to drink at a waterhole. Wild budgerigars are nearly all green, but domesticated ones may be blue or yellow.

Cockatoos live in the forests of Australasia. They are popular cage birds, distinguishable from other parrots by the crest of feathers on the head.

(see page 37), but it is used mainly for cracking seeds. The top half of the beak is hinged near its base, giving tremendous crushing power to the beak as a whole. The macaws of South America have no trouble in cracking the extremely hard Brazil nuts, and if you put out a finger to a macaw it could snap it off with a single bite. The beak also has another important job: it acts as a third foot, clinging to branches while the bird climbs.

There are two major groups of parrots – those with thick, blunt tongues, and those with brush-tipped tongues. The latter group contains the lories and lorikeets of Australasia. These birds have slender, wavy-edged beaks and they use their tongues to mop up nectar and fruit juices. Lorikeets often do serious damage in orchards because they crush and destroy the flowers in order to lap up the nectar. The kea, from the uplands of New Zealand, is a large brush-tongued parrot with some strange habits. During the summer it feeds mainly on nectar, but in the winter digs up insects and also eats dead animals. It is attracted to sheep-farming regions where sometimes it kills sick or injured sheep by standing on their backs and using its wickedly sharp beak to tear them open and eat their flesh.

The blunt-tongued parrots feed mainly on buds, seeds, and fruits. Some of the smaller species, commonly known as parakeets, live on the grasslands and they are serious pests in the grain fields of Africa and Australia. The budgerigar is the best known of these grain feeders. It lives in vast flocks on the Australian plains. Several of the parakeets of south east Asia are called hanging parakeets because of their habit of sleeping hanging upside down, just like the bats.

Most parrots are very fond of company and they normally go about in flocks, filling the air with their shrill screams and squawks. During the breeding season there is a great deal of noisy courtship behaviour as the birds get to know each other. Many of the species mate for life, and once paired up they are always together. Nowhere is this more obvious than among the lovebirds of Africa. These birds spend hours sitting together and preening each other, or simply rubbing their beaks together in a prolonged kiss. It is sometimes said that if one of the pair dies the other will die from a broken heart.

The majority of parrots make their nests in holes in dead trees where they lay white, almost spherical eggs. There is no need for coloured eggs in a dark nest hole.

The African grey parrot is the best 'talker' of them all. Like most of the larger parrots, it displays human-like behaviour in picking up its food in one foot and tasting it before eating.

An osprey swoops down to the water, talons outstretched to snatch a fish from the surface. Rough scales under the feet grip the slippery fish firmly.

A hovering kestrel. Its amazing eyesight allows it to pick out a grasshopper in the grass below.

Birds of prey

The birds of prey are flesh-eating birds with sharply hooked beaks and powerful claws or talons. There are two distinct groups: the hawks and eagles, which hunt by day, and the night-hunting owls. The two groups are not related and the similarities between them are simply due to the fact that both groups are adapted for hunting. Small mammals, especially rodents and birds, form their main food, but the smaller birds of prey also eat a lot of insects and some species eat fish. The secretary bird of Africa (see page 9) feeds mainly on snakes. Several species, notably the vultures, eat carrion (dead animals). All birds of prey are our allies because they destroy huge numbers of rats and other pests.

There are just over 200 different kinds of hawks and eagles, ranging from tiny falconets weighing only 35 grams to huge eagles and vultures with weights of 14 kilograms and wingspans of more than three metres. They hunt in different ways, but all have remarkably good eyesight. Vultures, buzzards, and many eagles soar high in the air, their broad wings keeping them safely aloft on currents of rising air. They drop down quickly when they see food on the ground. The harriers and falcons have narrow wings and fly quickly. Harriers swoop to and fro low over the ground in their search for food, while most falcons race after birds in mid-air. Sparrowhawks and other forest-living birds of prey generally have rather short wings and long, rudder-like tails. This gives them wonderful manoeuvrability through the trees and branches.

All birds of prey usually kill with their feet, as can be seen from the toes which are strongly clawed and very powerful in most species. The exceptions are the vultures. These birds eat carrion and have no need for murderous talons. Vultures normally live in rather open habitats, where they can see the ground from high in the air. They are particularly associated with mountains and deserts. The largest of all the vultures is the magnificent Andean condor from the Andes mountains of South America. Vultures are very important 'dustmen', rapidly disposing of dead animals and clearing up the scraps after lions and other animals have fed. They leave only the skin and bone, and several beetles then come along to dispose of this. Some vultures do actually manage to deal with bones although they have no teeth. They take them up into the air and drop them onto rocks until they break. The vultures can then reach the nourishing marrow. The Egyptian vulture has another clever trick for getting the contents out of ostrich eggs. It picks up a small stone in its beak and hurls it at the egg over and over again until the egg breaks.

Owls

Although the little owl can often be seen swooping over the fields and looking for insects by day, the majority of the owls hunt at night. Their huge, forward-looking eyes enable them to see very well in the moonlight, although they hunt by ear as much as by eye. Their feathers are very soft, enabling the birds to fly almost silently. This means that they can hear the slightest rustle of a mouse in the grass and swoop down on it without the mouse hearing its approach. The owls are not always silent, however, and give out a wide variety of eerie calls when they start to hunt in the evening. Like the songs of other birds, these calls indicate ownership of territory and tell other owls to keep away from the hunting ground. The calls are also used during courtship, together with some strange dancing and posing.

Owls rest in trees and old buildings by day and, although often beautifully camouflaged, they give their position away by dropping their pellets. These consist of the fur and bones and other indigestible parts of the owls' prey. The owls spit out these pellets quite regularly and, by examining them, you can see what the birds had for dinner. Other birds of prey also produce pellets, but these do not normally contain bones because hawks and eagles can digest the bony parts of their victims.

A long-eared owl returns to its perch with a rat.

The bald head and neck of a vulture (left) might look ugly, but baldness is essential for a bird which plunges its head into rotting carcases. A feathered head (right) would soon be ruined.

A peregrine falcon 'stooping' at great speed after a pigeon. Peregrines are among the fastest of all birds, with diving speeds of 130 kph

A gannet (left) plunges into the water for a fish.

are white in colour. They often nest in immense colonies, usually on remote cliffs and islands. The gannet is one of these colonial nesters, with each seaweed nest less than a metre from the next. The birds bring back so much nourishing fish and squid from the sea that the young gannets get too heavy to fly properly. They stumble to the edge of the cliff and then glide down to the water. They then have to swim about without food until they lose enough weight to be able to take off. Flying over the waves at heights of perhaps 30 metres, the birds see

A cormorant swimming under water after a shoal of fishes. Unlike other sea birds, the cormorant does not have completely waterproof plumage and when it gets back to land after a dive it hangs its wings out to dry.

Birds of the sea

Seagulls are familiar to everyone who goes to the seaside. They soar and glide above the waves and the beach, dropping down every now and then to snatch up a stranded crab or a discarded sandwich. They also follow ships far out to sea to feed on the scraps that are thrown overboard, and they go far inland to feed at rubbish dumps and to follow the plough for worms. The gulls are real scavengers and their stout beaks can deal with almost any kind of food.

But gulls are only one of many groups of birds that live on or by the sea. Most of these birds have webbed feet, which help them to swim and to walk on soft mud, and many of them

A puffin returns to its burrow with a beakful of fish for its nestling.

fishes below the surface and plunge down to catch them with spectacular dives.

The puffin swims around on the surface until it sees some fishes, and it then dives after them. It uses its wings as paddles under the water and usually comes up with several fishes in its beak. Cormorants also swim well under water, and Japanese fishermen have trained them to bring fish back to the boat. A collar round the bird's neck prevents it from

Gulls (left) and an albatross (top right) soaring over a ship.

Frigate birds (below) attacking a booby and making it drop its food, which the frigate birds immediately snatch up.

swallowing the fish, and a line attached to the collar prevents the bird from escaping.

The largest of the sea birds is the wandering albatross, whose narrow wings span nearly 3·5 metres. It goes out to sea for months on end and roams all over the southern oceans searching for fish and squid. Following a zig-zag course, first into the wind to gain height, and then turning to glide downwind, the bird can remain airborne for hours without ever flapping its wings.

The frigate birds or man-o'-war birds of tropical seas are also wonderful aeronauts, swooping down to snatch fish from the surface without even getting their feathers wet. They are called man-o'-war birds because they often turn pirate and chase other birds and make them drop their food.

The birds described so far all go out to sea to feed, but there are many more that feed on the shore. These are the wading birds. They have relatively long legs and they wander about in shallow water or on the sand and mud, probing for worms and shellfish with their long, slender beaks. They include oystercatchers, redshanks, sandpipers, and many others. They are generally more numerous on the shore in autumn and winter, for many of them breed on marshland away from the coast.

The oystercatcher probes the mud for shellfish.

The tufted duck (left) takes off by running along the surface. Dabbling ducks, such as the mallard (right), take off simply by jumping into the air.

Birds of fresh water

Freshwater birds can be conveniently divided into those which sit on the surface and swim and those which simply wade in the shallows. The main group of swimmers are the ducks and their relatives. These all have webbed feet which they use as paddles to push themselves through the water. Their legs are short, however, and the birds all waddle rather clumsily on land. All have flattened beaks with sieve-like arrangements around the edge to strain food from the water.

The ducks have rather short necks and the males, called drakes, are often much more brightly coloured than the females. This is easily seen in the common mallard which lives on lakes and rivers everywhere: the female is a drab brown but the drake has a beautiful green head and chestnut breast. The mallard belongs to a group called dabbling ducks. These feed on submerged plants and small animals, which they collect by sticking their heads under the water. Sometimes they completely up-end themselves and dabble on the bottom with just the tail above water, but they do not submerge completely. The diving ducks, such as the pochard, dive right down into the water to feed. These ducks live on more open water than the dabblers and often go out to sea.

Geese are closely related to ducks, but they have longer necks and the males and females are very similar. They feed mainly on grass and other waterside vegetation. The swans also belong to the same group, but they are larger than geese and their necks are even longer and more slender. The mute swan is probably the heaviest flying bird in the world, with weights of about 16 kilograms being quite common. Swans sometimes graze like geese, but more often they feed in the water like ducks. Like some of the geese, they mate for life and there are strong family ties be-

A family of mute swans. Both parents are very protective, and the male (left) is threatening an intruder.

tween parents and the young cygnets. Swans and geese, like most of the ducks, nest on the ground close to the water. They lay quite a lot of eggs and the young birds are able to swim almost as soon as they hatch. Outside the breeding season, the birds often live in large flocks. This is especially true of those species that migrate. Huge numbers of ducks, geese, and swans fly south from the Arctic regions in autumn to spend the winter in the less cold parts of Europe and North America.

The grebes belong to quite a different family of water birds. When swimming, they can be distinguished by their very upright necks and pointed beaks. Their feet are not webbed, but flaps of skin on the edges of their toes serve the same function as the webbing. Grebes are excellent divers and they often disappear without warning, only to surface several yards away with a beakful of plant or animal food. They sometimes swim with the body submerged and the head sticking out of

During the strange courtship of the great crested grebe each bird dives down and comes up with some water weed which it presents to its partner.

All change: a moorhen leaves its nest, with its mate standing by to take over the incubation.

the water like a periscope. Grebes hardly ever come ashore, and they make floating nests from water plants. They perform long and elaborate courtship dances before building their nests.

Coots and moorhens belong to yet another family of water birds. They do not have webbed feet, although the coot has flaps on its toes like the grebes. The common coot is black, with a prominent white patch on its face. The moorhen cannot fly well and it swims rather slowly and jerkily. It lives on overgrown ponds and in ditches where there is plenty of cover in which to hide.

Several kinds of long-legged wading birds visit the edges of ponds and streams to feed, and some nest there as well. Herons, bitterns, and pelicans are well-known waterside birds. The pelican uses its huge beak like a fishing net to catch food. Flamingos stand on one leg for hours on end, and they feed with their heads completely upside down. In this way, they can sift food from the mud without getting their beautiful feathers dirty.

Flamingos having a noisy argument about who stands where. The diagram shows how the birds feed with their heads completely upside down.

Feathered jewels

The most colourful birds are found in the tropical regions, particularly in the forested areas, and none is brighter than the little hummingbirds of the Americas. These include the smallest of all birds – the bee hummingbird, which is only five or six centimetres long and shorter than some bumble bees. Not all of the 300 or so species are brightly coloured, and it is usually only the males that have the splendid robes. They have beautiful metallic sheens on most parts of the body and they are often decorated with long 'beards' and 'moustaches'. Many also have long, curved tail feathers, some of which look like stout wires with flags on the ends. These decorations are all used to impress the females during the marvellous aerial courtship dances. The wings may beat as much as 200 times a second at such times, although they normally beat between 50 and 100 times a second. This is still very fast and it gives out the hum for which the birds are named.

Hummingbirds dart about with amazing speed and they can even hover and fly backwards. They usually hover while feeding at flowers, and the Portuguese name for the birds means 'kiss-the-flower'. The birds use their long beaks and tongues to probe deeply into the flowers to suck up the nectar. Some of them have bristly tongue tips which they use to pick up small insects in the flowers. The beak in some species is longer than the whole body.

Although most common in the forests of Colombia and Ecuador, the hummingbirds are not entirely confined to the tropics. During the summer they spread as far north as Alaska, but move back to a warmer climate for the winter. It is amazing that these tiny birds can migrate over such huge distances. For their size, the male hummingbirds are aggressive and frequently dive at larger ani-

(Above left), a hummingbird hovers at a flower and plunges its long tongue in to get nectar. Another bird sits on her tiny nest. (Below left), a toucan uses its huge beak to gather fruit, and it also uses it in courtship displays.

mals to frighten them away, although the birds usually swerve at the last moment and do not actually hit their targets.

The birds of paradise are much larger than the hummingbirds, but the males are similarly adorned with ornate feathers. Large numbers were once killed to provide decorations for ladies' hats, and several species became rare. Feathers are still used in native ceremonies in New Guinea, where most of the birds of paradise live, but export of the birds is banned. The birds of paradise perform their

A brightly coloured male bird of paradise dancing and displaying his extravagant plumage to the drab hen bird.

courtship dances on the ground or on branches, and several males often put on a show together. Some of the species actually make a 'stage' by clearing the leaves and twigs from the dancing area, and some even remove overhanging leaves so that the sun can shine down like a spotlight onto the dancers. The birds then pair up and mate but, as in the hummingbirds, the gaudy males take no part in building the nests or rearing the young. This is left entirely to the drab-looking females – a much safer arrangement, because the colourful males would soon draw attention to the nest.

The bower birds of Australia and New Guinea are related to the birds of paradise, but they are not so gaily adorned. Nevertheless, the males put on a colourful display to attract the females. They build courting houses called bowers and decorate them with colourful flowers, fruits, pebbles, and even buttons and bottle tops when they can find them. Some lay carpets of moss in and around their bowers, and some even produce dyes by chewing up fruits and daubing the liquid over the bower with pieces of grass or bark. The bowers themselves are of several different types. Some, called avenue bowers, consist of two parallel rows of twigs, often arched over to form a simple tunnel. Others are like small gardens fenced with twigs, while some are miniature grass huts built around the bases of small trees.

The female bower bird is first attracted by the male's song. He then shows her the bower and, by offering her various pieces of the decoration, he encourages her to enter. If she finds things to her liking, the birds will continue their courtship and will eventually mate. The female will then go away and build a nest and rear her young by herself.

A male satin bower bird using a piece of bark as a paintbrush to decorate his bower.

The Nile crocodile happily allows Egyptian plovers to peck leeches from its gums – a remarkable partnership.

Crocodiles and other reptiles

The reptiles are cold-blooded, backboned animals whose bodies are almost always covered with scales. Living reptiles include crocodiles, turtles, snakes, and lizards, but these are all rather insignificant compared with the huge dinosaurs of the past. These magnificent creatures, some of them 25 metres long, dominated the earth for over 100 million years, but they died out more than 70 million years ago and left only the relatively small reptiles that we have around us today. There are about 6,000 living species, found mainly in the tropical regions. They live on land, in fresh water, and in the sea, but they never dominate the scene as did the dinosaurs. Mammals, birds, and fishes all play a much bigger role in today's habitats than the reptiles.

The largest living reptiles, and the nearest relatives of the dinosaurs, are the crocodilians, which include crocodiles, alligators, caimans, and the odd-looking gavial. They are found only in the warmer parts of the world. They spend most of their time floating in the water or sun-bathing on the river banks, but most can move surprisingly quickly when necessary, both on land and in the water.

There are about 25 species of crocodilians, but only two of these are true alligators. The American alligator lives in the south eastern United States and reaches lengths of more than five metres, while the Chinese alligator from the Yangtse River is not much more than one metre long. Alligators are much more lethargic than crocodiles and much less aggressive and dangerous.

The caimans of tropical America are closely related to the alligators, but differ in having bony plates embedded in the skin of the belly. They are much more aggressive than alligators, often snapping their powerful jaws and hissing loudly as soon as anything approaches. The largest of the five species is the black caiman, with a length of up to five metres. Caimans and alligators have blunter snouts than crocodiles, but the two groups are best separated by their teeth. The crocodile's teeth

A crocodile's head showing the fourth tooth in the lower jaw sticking up on the outside of the upper jaw. In some old animals these teeth have fallen out.

The snout of an alligator tends to be broader than that of a crocodile. When the mouth is shut the fourth tooth in the lower jaw fits into a socket in the upper jaw.

To catch its food the fish-eating gavial swings its toothy jaws through the water.

are nearly all visible when its mouth is shut, and the fourth tooth in the lower jaw is prominent, sticking up like a tusk on the outside of the crocodile's snout. In alligators and caimans this tooth is concealed in a pit in the upper jaw when the mouth is closed, and the other teeth are more or less hidden as well. Crocodiles are found in all tropical regions and, unlike alligators, they often go out to sea. The Nile crocodile, which is found nearly all over Africa, is the best known species. It sometimes reaches lengths of about six metres, but the largest and most dangerous crocodile is the estuarine crocodile from south east Asia and New Guinea. Sizes are often exaggerated, but there is an authentic record of an estuarine crocodile just over eight metres long. This beast must have weighed about two tonnes.

Crocodiles and alligators all lead very similar lives. During the mating season the males roar and bellow loudly, often fighting among themselves and inflicting terrible injuries with their teeth and thrashing tails. After mating, the females lay lots of eggs in pits or else in piles of rotting leaves. The females stay by their 'nests' and uncover the eggs when they hear the babies starting to break out. The babies may stay with their mothers for a day or two, but they soon disperse. They eat frogs, insects, and other small animals at first, but they start to eat fishes as they get larger. Adult crocodilians eat fishes, but their main food is probably mammals and birds which are caught when they come down to the water to drink.

Above: Young crocodiles hatching from their eggs. Their mother may help them out of the nest, but she does nothing else for them.

Right: Male alligators carrying on one of their very noisy fights.

Reptiles with shells

The shelled reptiles are the turtles and tortoises, all easily recognized by the box-like shells in which their bodies are encased. Soft-shelled turtles have leathery shells, but the typical shell consists of a number of bony plates covered with patches of horny tortoise-shell. Those species which live in the sea are generally called turtles, while the land-living species are usually called tortoises. Those that live in fresh water may also be called turtles, but they are often referred to as terrapins. None of the shelled reptiles or chelonians is completely adapted for life in the water, for all breathe air and all have to come on to land to lay their eggs.

None of the 200 or so species of chelonians has any teeth, but the animals all have a tough beak for grasping and biting their food. The head can be pushed quite a long way out of the shell to gather food, but it can be almost completely withdrawn when the animal is resting or frightened. Most of the species withdraw the head by bending the neck vertically like a letter S, but a few bend the neck sideways to bring the head in. The legs of some species can also be withdrawn for safety. With the ribs firmly fixed to the shell, the animals cannot breathe in the normal way. Muscles in the stomach region have taken over from the chest muscles to pump air in and out of the lungs.

The legs of the marine turtles have become modified into broad, flat flippers and the animals use them just like wings to 'fly' through the water at surprisingly high speeds. The front flippers of the leathery turtle, or luth, span nearly four metres in some specimens. This animal reaches lengths of over two metres and weights of more than 700 kilograms, making it by far the largest of the living chelonians. The luth has no real bony shell – just a few small plates of bone embedded in its thick, leathery skin. It feeds mainly on jellyfishes and other soft-bodied animals living near the surface. The green turtle feeds mainly on seaweed, but the other marine species are omnivorous creatures, eating large quantities of fish and crustaceans as well as seaweed.

Although marine turtles are found in most of the warmer seas, they have rather restricted

Top-left: A diamond-backed terrapin sunbathes on a log. Below: Green turtles lay lots of eggs in the sand, but few eggs grow into adult turtles. Most of the hatchlings are eaten by birds (right).

smaller species. It is sometimes possible to work out the age of a tortoise by counting the layers of tortoiseshell on its back. There is normally one layer for each year, but the older ones often get worn away.

Freshwater tortoises, or terrapins, have flatter bodies as a rule, but they cannot swim as well as the marine species. Most of them are carnivorous and some can give painful bites if they are picked up. The largest freshwater species is the alligator snapper of North America. It catches ducks with its large jaws and its head is too big to be pulled into the shell.

breeding areas and they always return to certain beaches to lay their eggs. Their flippers are not very efficient on the sand, and the females really have to struggle to get up the beach. They lay dozens of eggs in a hole and then leave them alone. Very few of the eggs produce adult turtles because they have so many enemies. Man takes large numbers of eggs for food, and this has made some of the turtles very rare.

Land tortoises are very slow-moving animals with high-domed shells and thick, scaly legs, although some desert-living species have spade-like front legs with which they dig out their burrows. Tortoises are all plant eaters, the desert species being quite happy to munch prickly cacti with their horny beaks. Giant tortoises weighing up to 200 kilograms occur on some remote islands such as the Galapagos Islands in the Pacific and the Aldabra Isles in the Indian Ocean. These tortoises can live for more than 100 years, and so can some of the

Top left: The matamata of northern Brazil lives in stagnant pools and its long neck allows it to breathe while it rests on the bottom of a shallow pool. Its strange shell, which is about 50 cm long, bears three rows of knobbly spikes. Above: The giant tortoise of the Galapagos Islands is feeding happily on prickly cacti. Giant tortoises are found only on remote islands where they have no natural competitors for food.

The Komodo dragon, which reaches lengths of three metres, is the largest living lizard. It lives only on a few small islands in Indonesia. It feeds on a variety of animals, and large individuals probably kill deer and pigs. Komodo dragons do not leave much behind when they have finished eating.

Lizards

The lizards are the most abundant of today's reptiles. There are about 3,000 species and they are found all over the world except for the very coldest parts. The most northerly species is the viviparous lizard, which extends beyond the Arctic Circle in Europe. The seaweed-eating marine iguana of the Galapagos Islands is the only lizard that goes into the sea, but lizards occur in almost every habitat on the land. Many live in the desert and they have evolved special behaviour to keep themselves cool. Some of them run on tiptoe and keep their bodies right off the hot sand. Some even stand right up and run only on the back legs: air blowing on to their bellies keeps them even cooler. Many of the desert lizards have fringes of scales on their toes to help them to run on the loose sand. Grasslands and forests have large numbers of lizards, and there are even 'flying lizards' in the trees. These animals do not really fly, but simply glide on outstretched flaps of skin like the flying lemurs (see page 32).

The largest lizard is the Komodo dragon, which may be three metres long. It belongs to a group of lizards called monitors. These are all flesh-eating creatures with rather long necks. Several other lizards exceed two metres in length, but the majority are less than half a metre long. Some of the large ones bite hard when handled, but only two lizards, both living in the deserts of North America, are actually poisonous.

The chameleons are strange lizards famous for their ability to change colour to match different backgrounds. Their eyes detect the general colour of the surroundings and the brain then sends signals to the body to alter the distribution of the dark pigment in the skin. By changing this distribution, the chameleon can vary from yellow, through green and blue to brown and black. Chameleons also have remarkably long tongues, which they can flick out at lightning speed to pick up insects for food. In other respects, however, these lizards are extremely slow: their feet grip the branches very securely and a chameleon rarely moves one foot unless the other three are firmly attached. For even greater safety the tail can also grip the branch.

The gila monster is not actually very large, but it has a poisonous bite. Note the fat tail.

common iguana

flap-necked chameleon

skink

eyed lizard

Madagascan gecko

frilled lizard

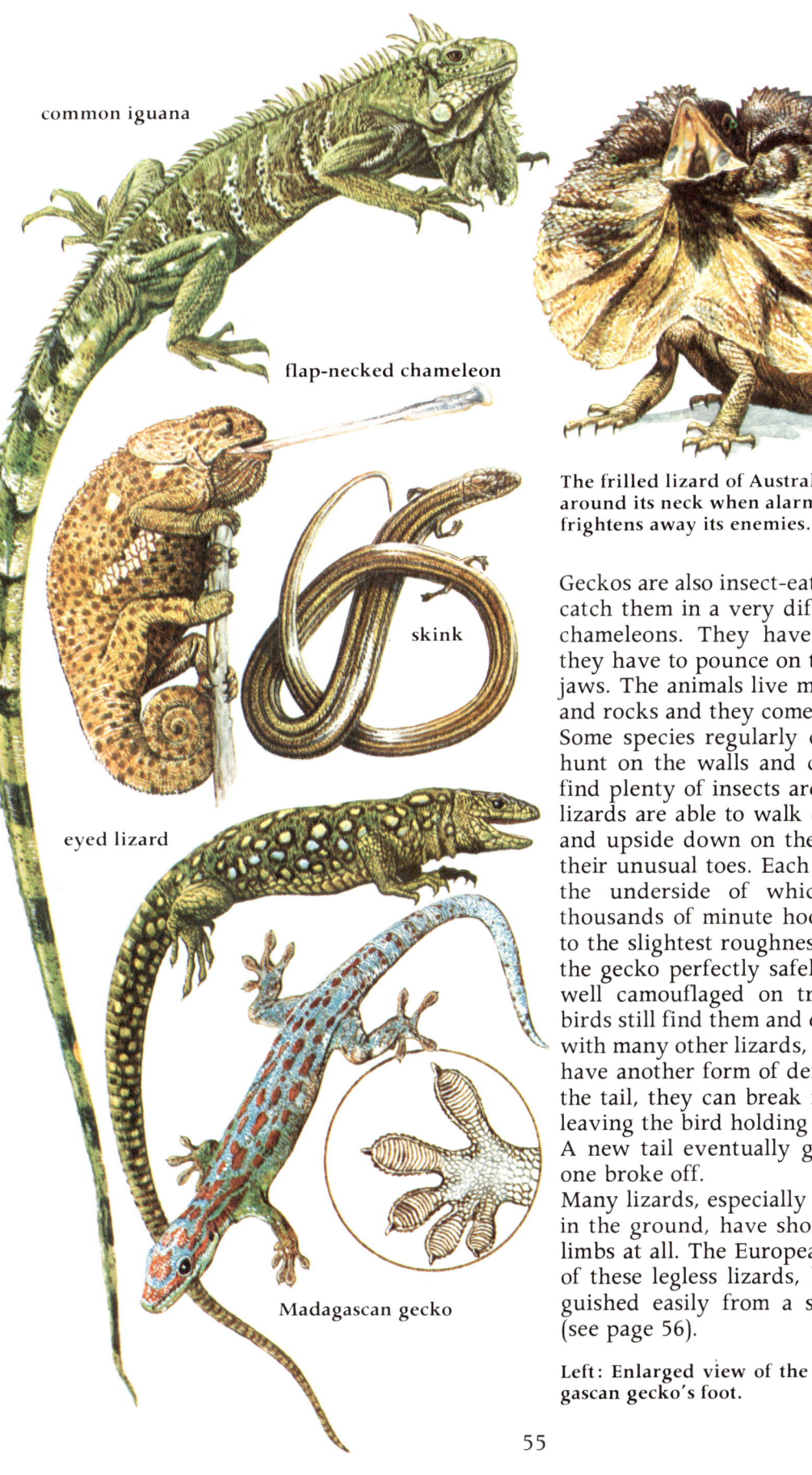

The frilled lizard of Australia opens the big collar around its neck when alarmed, and this generally frightens away its enemies.

Geckos are also insect-eating lizards, but they catch them in a very different way from the chameleons. They have short tongues and they have to pounce on their prey with their jaws. The animals live mainly on tree trunks and rocks and they come out to feed at night. Some species regularly come into houses to hunt on the walls and ceilings, where they find plenty of insects around the lights. The lizards are able to walk on the smooth walls and upside down on the ceilings because of their unusual toes. Each toe has a broad tip, the underside of which is clothed with thousands of minute hooks. These can cling to the slightest roughness of a wall and hold the gecko perfectly safely. Many geckos are well camouflaged on trees and rocks, but birds still find them and eat them. In common with many other lizards, however, the geckos have another form of defence. If grabbed by the tail, they can break it off and run away, leaving the bird holding just a wriggling tail. A new tail eventually grows where the old one broke off.

Many lizards, especially those which burrow in the ground, have short limbs, or even no limbs at all. The European slow-worm is one of these legless lizards, but it can be distinguished easily from a snake by its eyelids (see page 56).

Left: Enlarged view of the underside of a Madagascan gecko's foot.

The snakes

Snakes evolved many millions of years ago from lizards which lived under the ground. Some primitive snakes still live in the soil today, but others have spread into different habitats and, despite having no legs, they are a very successful group of reptiles. Most of them live on the ground, but some have taken to life in the trees and several species lead their entire lives in the sea. Most of the 2,600 or so species live in the tropics, but the European viper or adder reaches right up to the Arctic Circle. Like all reptiles in cool regions, it hibernates through the winter.

The animals have mastered the problems of moving without legs very successfully. Many of them use the scales on the belly like numerous feet. The scales are moved forward in turn and dug into the ground, and the snake pulls itself forward in a smooth glide. The animal is helpless on a smooth, hard surface which provides no grip for the scales. The other major method of getting about involves bending the body into S-shaped loops. By pushing the loops back against stones and other objects, the snake forces its whole body forward.

Below: The diagrams below show the enormous gape of the viper's mouth. In one drawing the fangs are being pushed into a rubber-topped cup to collect the poison. The snake-charmer's cobra (above) is actually responding to the movements of the charmer and not to the noise he is making.

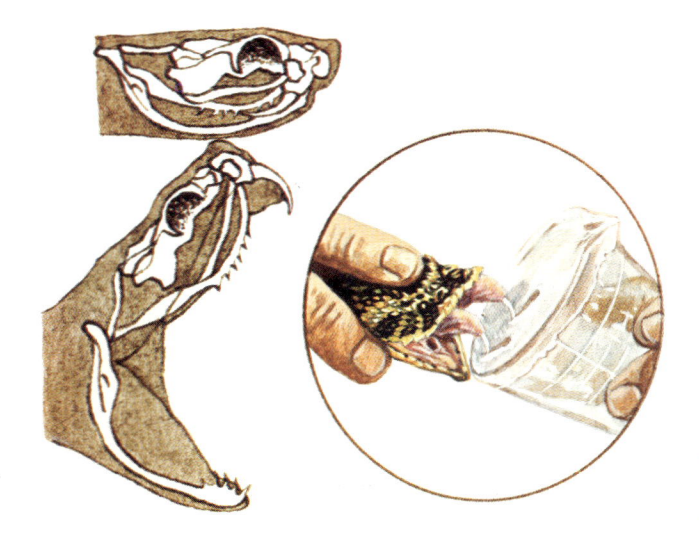

Snakes have no eardrums and they do not hear ordinary sounds very well, but they do have internal ears and they are very sensitive to vibrations of the ground. The animals also have no eyelids, giving them their well-known glassy stare. Their eyes are protected by tough layers of transparent skin called the spectacle. It does not matter if this gets scratched as the animals slither about, because all snakes shed the outer layer of their skins every few weeks and the outer layer of the spectacle comes off too.

As it moves about, a snake continually flicks its tongue in and out. This is its way of smelling out food. The tongue picks up particles of scent and carries them back to the mouth where they are examined, just as we examine scents with our noses.

Snakes are all carnivorous. Most of them eat relatively small animals, such as frogs and insects, which they simply grab with their numerous backward-pointing teeth. These teeth cannot bite or chew and the prey is always swallowed whole. The largest snakes – the pythons and boas – belong to the group called constrictors. They grab their prey and

Top: The diamond rattlesnake displays its rattle, which is made from horny pieces of skin.
Centre: The egg-eating snake engulfs a whole egg. Inside the mouth, the shell cracks and only the yolk is swallowed.

twine their powerful bodies around it until it suffocates. The largest of these snakes is the anaconda of South America, which sometimes exceeds 10 metres in length.

Poisonous snakes use venom to paralyse their prey before swallowing it. They strike rapidly and inject the poison with special teeth called fangs. These may be at the front of the mouth or at the back. The front-fanged species, such as the cobras, mambas, and rattlesnakes, are the most dangerous. The largest of them is the king cobra of south east Asia, which may be nearly six metres long. There are actually only about 150 really dangerous snakes in the world. The only poisonous species in the British Isles is the viper.

Because of their unusual jaws, snakes can swallow enormous meals, much fatter than their own bodies. The two halves of the lower jaw can be separated at the front, and the whole jaw can be detached from the skull. The skin is very elastic and the mouth can open extremely wide. Using its teeth like grappling hooks, the snake can pull its mouth right over its prey and engulf it. This is a slow job, however, and the snake has to push its windpipe right to the front of its mouth so that it can continue to breathe while swallowing its meal.

Below: The reticulated python, one of the world's largest snakes, is starting to swallow a wild pig which it has squeezed to death. It may take some hours to swallow the whole animal.

The amphibians

Newts, salamanders, frogs, and toads all belong to the class of backboned animals called amphibians. This name means 'double-life', and it is very apt because most of the amphibians spend part of their lives in water and part on land. They are cold-blooded animals and their skins are always moist. Except for a few strange legless and worm-like species called apodans, they have no scales in their skins.

Apart from the apodans, there are two major groups of amphibians. The newts and salamanders have long tails and most of them have four short legs. The frogs and toads, on the other hand, have no tails and they have powerful jumping legs. Although most of the adult amphibians live on land, they are still confined to damp places. Their skins are not waterproof and the animals dry up easily. They also suffocate in dry air because they absorb a lot of their oxygen through the thin skin and the skin must be moist for this absorption to take place. In addition, most amphibian species have to go back to water to breed.

Newts spend the summer in damp places, and in cool climates they hibernate for the winter. They wake up in the spring and head for the water. The males have frilled tails and attractive crests on the back at this time, and their bellies are brightly coloured. The males then dance in front of the females and the animals eventually pair up. The females lay their eggs singly on the water plants, taking care to fold the leaves over so as to conceal each egg.

The little newts that emerge from the eggs are called tadpoles. Instead of breathing air like the adults, they absorb oxygen from the water through tufts of feathery gills on the sides of the body. They feed on a variety of small water animals and after about four months they are ready to change into small newts. The gills disappear and the animals start to breathe air into their newly formed lungs. They crawl out of the water and begin

Above: Courting common newts, with the male (left) displaying his attractive tail and belly colours to the drab, plump female.

Below: The female newt lays her eggs on water plants; the tadpoles develop in the eggs; and then swim freely out into the water.

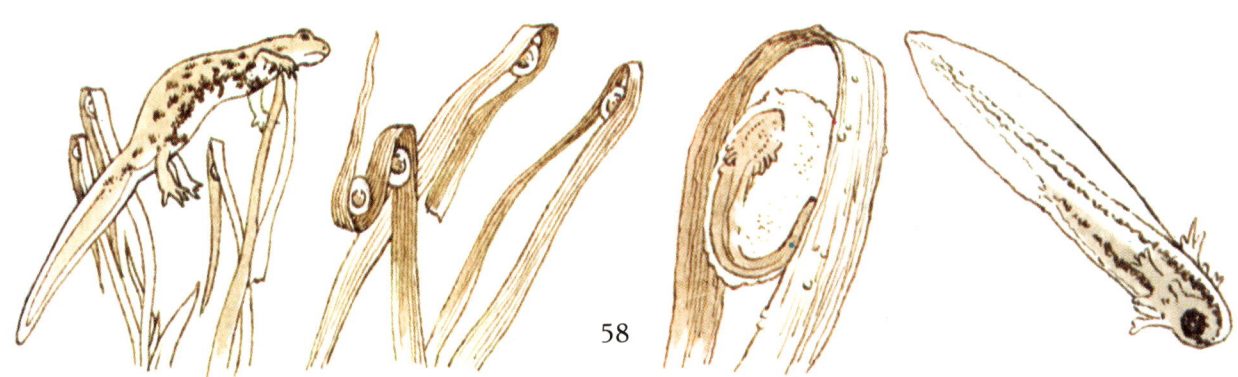

to eat slugs and insects, but take another three or four years to reach adult size.

Salamanders are newt-like animals, but they are generally better adapted than newts for life on land. Some have life histories like that of the newts, but there are many variations. Fire salamanders pair up on land and the females keep their eggs in their bodies until they hatch. The females then enter the water and give birth to the tadpoles. Some other salamanders have modified their life histories in such a way that they do not have to go into the water at all. They lay large eggs in damp places and the tadpoles complete their development inside the eggs. When the animals finally leave the eggs they are miniature salamanders and not tadpoles at all. It is as if each tadpole has a little pond all to itself inside its own egg. Although these salamanders do not have to enter the water, they are still confined to damp places because of their thin skins.

Some salamanders actually spend all their lives in the water. Among them is the Japanese giant salamander. With a length of more than one and a half metres and a weight of about 40 kilograms, this monster is the largest of all the amphibians. It eats fishes, frogs, and other aquatic animals.

A few salamanders never grow up completely: they stay in the water and keep their gills all their lives. They grow up in other ways, however, and lay eggs in the normal way. The Mexican axolotl is one of the most famous of these Peter Pan animals. It seems that in its native home a shortage of iodine in the water prevents it from growing up, for it can be made to turn into a salamander by adding a small amount of iodine.

Below: The Japanese giant salamander eating a fish. This, the largest of amphibians spends all of its time in the water.

Above: The strange Mexican axolotl, showing the feathery gills which it keeps for all its life.

Above: An olm is a blind salamander that lives in underground rivers in Southern Europe. It is about 30 cm long.

Above: The common or fire salamander.

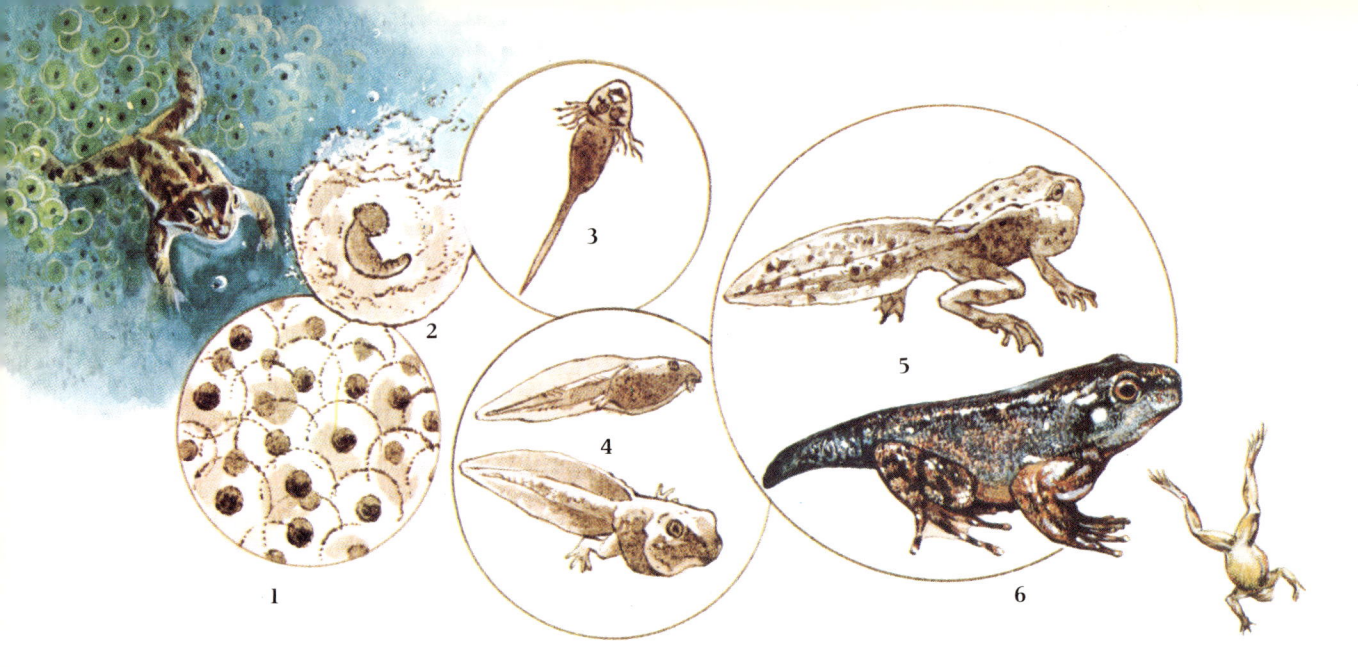

Frogs and toads

The life cycle of the common frog, from the time that the spawn is laid (1), through the various tadpole stages, to the small froglet (6).

The frogs and toads are mainly jumping amphibians with powerful back legs. These legs, with their large webbed feet, are also used in swimming. The common frog has a smooth, glistening skin, while the common toad has a rough, warty skin. As a result, we usually call all smooth-skinned species frogs and all rough-skinned species toads, but this is not a very scientific division. Tree frogs, for example, are more closely related to the toad than to the common frog.

Some adults spend their entire lives in the water and breathe entirely through the skin. They have no lungs. Most adults live on land, however, and feed on slugs and other small animals. The prey is caught by a very unusual tongue which is fixed at the front of the mouth instead of at the back. It has a sticky tip and it can be flicked out at very high speed to catch flies and other active insects. The water-dwelling toads are nearly all tongueless and they snap up their prey with their jaws.

Most frogs and toads live on the ground in marshy places, but many live high up in forest trees. Little suction pads on their toes help them to cling safely to shiny leaves. These tree frogs often catch flying insects by leaping up and grabbing them in mid air. Flying frogs actually glide from tree to tree,

The male midwife toad with the eggs on his legs.

Tiny toadlets emerge from the back of the Surinam toad.

60

A tree frog, showing the characteristic pads on its toes, shoots out its long and sticky tongue to snare an unwary fly.

borne up by the large webs that have developed on all four feet.

Some frogs and toads even manage to live in the desert. This seems very strange for animals which cannot live without water, but they have modified their life histories so that they are active only during the rainy season. For most of the year they hide deep underground where conditions remain moist.

In the breeding season the male frogs and toads are very noisy. Some of them inflate great pouches in their throats to amplify their calls, many of which have beautiful bell-like tones. Some can be heard more than a kilometre away. The females are attracted by the calls and the animals pair up. The males are smaller than the females and often ride around on their backs for a while. The eggs are then laid and a layer of jelly round each egg immediately swells up to produce the familiar spawn. The common frog lays all her eggs in one shapeless mass, while the common toad lays hers in long strings. As you can see in the picture, the tadpoles that hatch from the spawn are very different from the adults. They feed on water plants at first, and then take animal food as well. Whereas newt tadpoles keep their feathery gills until they are ready to leave the water, frog and toad tadpoles soon replace theirs with internal gills like those of fishes (see page 62). The tadpoles take about three months to turn into little frogs.

As with the salamanders, there are many variations on this basic life history. The midwife toad lays her string of eggs on land and the male then winds the string around his back legs. In dry weather he may give the eggs a dip in a puddle to keep them moist, but he does not normally go into the water until the eggs are about to hatch. The tadpoles can then swim away and grow up normally. The Surinam toad's eggs are pressed into the soft skin of her back as soon as they are laid. Each egg rests in a little pool, and a lid of skin grows over each one. The eggs hatch and the tadpoles remain in their pools for about three months. They then turn into tiny toads and hop out of their pouches. Mouth-breeding frogs of South America actually keep their tadpoles in their voice pouches until they turn into little frogs. In each of these examples, the tadpoles feed only on the yolk provided in the eggs.

Many frogs and toads have poison glands in their skin; the poison prevents other animals from eating them. Some of the most poisonous species are very brightly coloured. Their enemies learn to recognize these colours and patterns and leave the frogs alone. The bright colours and patterns are called warning colours. Some of the brightly coloured South American species are called arrow-poison frogs because the American Indians poison the tips of their hunting arrows with juices from the skins.

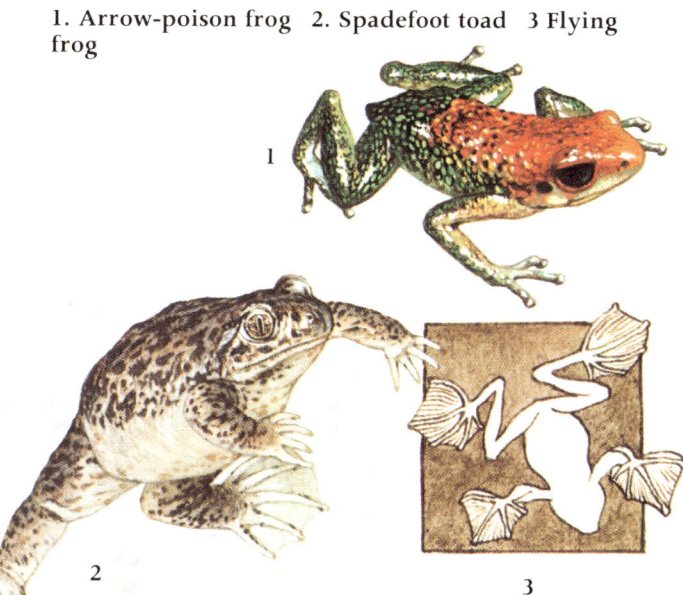

1. Arrow-poison frog 2. Spadefoot toad 3 Flying frog

The cod (top) and the blue shark show very well the differences in the fins and gills of the bony fishes and the sharks. The two mermaid's purses are those of the skate (left) and the common dogfish.

Introducing the fishes

A fish's body is designed for a life spent entirely under the water. Most fishes are streamlined, and to drive them through the water have a muscular tail that beats from side to side. Two pairs of fins, which correspond to the legs of land animals, are usually used for steering and braking, while other fins on the top and bottom of the body help to keep the fish on an even keel.

Most fishes get all their oxygen direct from the water by way of their gills and they do not have to surface for air. The gills consist of thousands of delicate 'fingers' hanging in pouches on each side of the throat. The pouches open into the throat and also to the outside of the body. Each gill finger or filament has extremely thin skin and contains lots of fine blood vessels. If you have ever watched fishes, you will know that they are always opening and closing their mouths. This is their way of breathing. Having taken a mouthful of water, the fish shuts its mouth and forces the water through the gill pouches. Some of the oxygen in the water passes through the thin skin of the gills and into the blood. Fishes cannot live in polluted water because it does not contain enough dissolved oxygen.

Despite being built for life in the water, some fishes can survive short periods out of water. Eels, for example, often slither across country from one stream to another. They breathe through their skins at such times, rather like the amphibians. Unlike most fishes, the eels do not have scaly coverings, and so oxygen can pass into the skin without trouble. The lungfishes of the tropics have real lungs as well as gills. They live in muddy backwaters and regularly gulp air into their lungs. Most of them can survive in burrows in the mud if the rivers dry up, and one species actually drowns if it cannot get to the surface to breathe air.

Living fishes fall into three main groups. The largest group, with more than 19,000 of the 20,000 or so known species, are the bony fishes. These have skeletons of real bone and most have delicate, fan-like fins. You can read about some of the bony fishes on the

The drawing shows how water goes in through the fish's mouth and out over the gills.

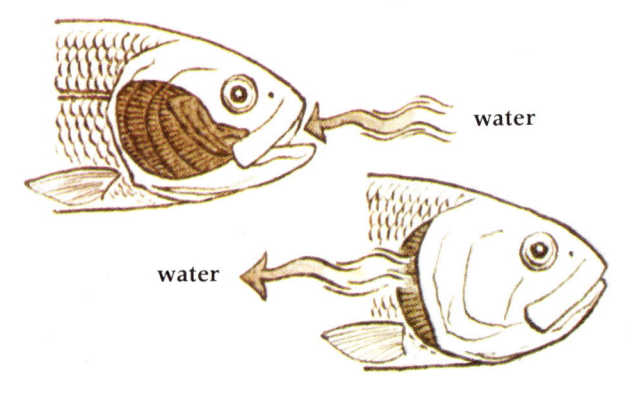

next four pages. The lampreys and hagfishes are eel-like creatures belonging to the group called cyclostomes. This name means 'round-mouths', for the animals have a circular mouth and no jaws. Teeth around the mouth scrape flesh from other fishes' bodies and this food is then sucked into the mouth.

The sharks and rays form the third group of fishes and are called elasmobranchs. Their skeletons are made of cartilage, which is tough and gristly but much softer than bone. These fishes all live in the sea. They differ visibly from bony fishes because their fins are covered with skin and there are five separate gill slits on each side. In bony fishes the gill openings are covered by a flap called the operculum, leaving just one visible opening on each side. Shark skins are very rough because they are covered with sharp scales. The scales on the lips are very large and sharp and they form the shark's formidable teeth. Some of the large sharks are very dangerous flesh-eaters, but the two largest species – the whale shark and the basking shark – feed by straining small animals from the water like the whalebone whales (see page 31). A sieve-like arrangement in the throat holds back the food as the water flows into the gill chambers. These huge sharks – the whale shark may be 20 metres long – have small teeth and they are harmless. Rays and skates are very flat fishes that normally feed on shellfish on the sea bed. They have broad, flat teeth designed for crushing shells instead of tearing flesh.

Thresher sharks working co-operatively to round up some smaller fishes for food.

Above: The black goby lives in coastal waters and makes a nest under sea shells.

Below: The manta ray or devil-fish is the largest of the rays and, unlike most of its relatives, swims freely near the surface (left). It even breaks through to glide in the air on its huge wing-like fins.

Some fishes of the sea

Thousands of different kinds of fishes live in the sea, but they are not evenly distributed through the waters. Like land animals, each kind has its preferred habitat. Some fishes like warm water; others prefer colder seas; some live near the coasts and others roam far out to sea; some stay near the surface, while others live on the sea bed.

The surface-living or pelagic fishes are generally quite small and often live in vast shoals. Herring, mackerel, sprat, and pilchard are among the important fishes in this group. They feed on the small planktonic animals

Above: Flying fishes gliding on their enormous front fins. Right: Some more fishes from the surface layers – herrings (top), mackerel (centre), and tunny.

that drift in the surface layers. Huge quantities of these fishes are caught for human food. They are trapped in drift nets which hang down in the water like curtains. The mesh

Below left: An angler fish about to catch a rock goby investigating the 'bait' over its mouth. Below: A male seahorse 'giving birth' to his babies, which escape from a pouch on his belly.

The porcupine fish is normally quite small, but it swells up into a prickly ball when frightened.

is just the right size to hold the fishes firmly when they swim into the nets.

Surface-living fishes have dark backs and silvery bellies. Enemies looking up from below 'lose' the fishes against the bright surface, while the dark backs camouflage the fishes from above. Their major enemies are sea birds and the larger surface-living fishes such as the tunny, the barracuda, and some of the sharks. The flying fishes of the warmer seas escape from these enemies by leaping right out of the water. They swim rapidly 'uphill' towards the surface and shoot through into the air spreading their enormous front fins like wings. A last few flicks of the tail in the water gives them enough speed for take-off. They can glide through the air for more than half a minute and cover several hundred metres. Flying fishes sometimes land on the decks of ships, but normally they glide just above the waves.

Many important food fishes live lower down in the sea. These include the cod (see page 62), hake, haddock, whiting, ling, coal-fish or saithe (coley or rock-salmon when it gets into the fish shops), plaice, and sole. Most of these fishes feed in mid-water, where they catch other fishes, prawns, and squid. The haddock feeds mainly on worms and other animals on the sea bed. The plaice and sole also eat bottom-living animals, for they belong to the group known as flatfishes and they are beautifully adapted for life on the sea bed.

The skates and rays, which are cartilaginous fishes, are flattened from top to bottom, but the flatfishes are flattened from side to side and they lie on one side – usually the left, although some flatfishes lie on their right side. The fishes are not flat to start with, however, and they look quite normal when they emerge from their eggs. Like those of most fishes, the eggs float at the surface, and the young fishes stay there for a while and feed on the plankton. But they soon move to the bottom and a strange change takes place. The skull becomes twisted so that both eyes are on one side, and the fish then lies on the other side.

Many small fishes known as blennies and gobies live among the coastal rocks and seaweeds, but the most unusual of all the fishes is surely the little seahorse. It stands on its tail to swim and moves forward by waving its back fin. At rest, it often anchors itself by coiling its tail round some seaweed. The female seahorse lays her eggs into a pouch on the male's belly, and he then carries them around until they hatch. The baby seahorses pop out of the pouch one by one.

Most marine fishes are fairly dull in colour, but those living on the coral reefs are often extremely bright. Deep-sea fishes, living in total darkness, often have their own lanterns to help them find their food and mates. Some angler fishes dangle luminous 'bait' over their mouths and snap up the small fishes that come to try it.

The adult plaice rests on its left side, with both eyes on the right side. The young fish (inset) looks quite normal and swims freely.

Freshwater fishes

Most freshwater fishes, like their marine cousins, have definite likes and dislikes concerning the waters in which they live. Strong-swimming, muscular fishes such as trout prefer fast-flowing streams in hilly regions, while the tench and carp prefer still or very slow-moving water with a muddy bottom. Some fishes, however, are less fussy. The pike and the nine-spined stickleback, for example, are equally happy in weedy lakes and canals and in the brackish water of estuaries.

A few fishes actually migrate freely between the rivers and the sea. Some lampreys (page 63) and sticklebacks do this, but the most famous migrants are the eel and the salmon. European eels leave the rivers when they are mature and swim some 5,000 kilometres to the Sargasso Sea in the western Atlantic. They spawn there and die, but the baby eels make their way back across the Atlantic in the Gulf Stream. The journey takes them about three years, and then they go up the rivers and stay there for several years until they are fully grown and ready for the long trip back to the Sargasso. The salmon does things the other way round: it grows up in the sea and enters the rivers to lay its eggs. It prefers the upper reaches, where the bottom is gravelly, and it will make tremendous leaps to get over waterfalls and other obstacles on its way upstream. Many salmon die from exhaustion after laying their eggs because they do not feed while coming upstream. But some manage to get back to the sea and build up their strength. They go up the rivers to spawn again the next year.

A few freshwater fishes, such as the European bitterling, are almost entirely herbivorous, but most species take at least some animal food and many are purely carnivorous. The trout, for example, feeds on the insects that crawl about on the river bed or fly just over the surface. Worms, molluscs, and crustaceans are eaten by many fishes, and small fishes are regularly eaten by their larger cousins. The voracious pike, for example, eats a lot of roach, together with plenty of frogs and the occasional duckling. The infamous piranhas of tropical America normally feed on smaller fishes, but they sometimes attack larger animals and their razor-sharp teeth quickly

Above: The archer fish spits a stream of water droplets with amazing accuracy at an insect resting above the water. The insect falls down and is eaten by the fish. **Below:** The brightly coloured male stickleback 'dances' in front of the silvery female to attract her to his nest.

Above: Salmon leaping up a waterfall during their journey to the egg-laying grounds in the upper reaches of the river. Below: The mouth-brooding tilapia which, for safety, keeps its youngsters in its mouth.

strip all the flesh from it. A capybara (page 21) weighing about 45 kilograms was reduced to a skeleton by a pack of piranhas in less than one minute.

Several freshwater fishes are able to give out powerful electric shocks. These shocks are usually used to stun other fishes so that they can be caught and eaten, but they can also be used for defence and navigation. The electric eel of Amazonia can generate enough electricity to stun any animal walking through the water – even an animal as large as a horse. The little guppy, which is a favourite aquarium fish, is one of a number of freshwater fishes that give birth to active babies. Most fishes lay eggs, often in enormous numbers. A female tench, for example, can lay nearly a million eggs each spring. Large numbers are necessary because the eggs are usually abandoned and nearly all of them or the young fishes they produce get eaten. Those fishes which do look after their eggs and young lay fewer eggs. The male stickleback is a good father. He builds a small nest with water weeds and persuades one or more females to lay their eggs in it. He then looks after perhaps a thousand eggs, fanning them regularly to ensure that they get plenty of fresh, clean water.

Some tropical fishes called mouth-brooders actually carry their eggs in their mouths. The young fishes are also carefully shepherded by mother or father, or both, and if danger threatens the little fishes are quickly herded into their parents' mouths. The mouth-brooders have to learn very quickly to distinguish between their youngsters and their food.

Left: The African catfish swims upside down and gathers food from the surface. Below: The eel has already swum about 5,000 kilometres before it reaches the European river where it will grow up.

The octopus and the squid

The word octopus often conjures up visions of hideous sea monsters, but the animal does not really deserve such a reputation. Most of the 150 or so species have bodies no larger than your hand, and some are very attractive when they are moving. There are some larger species with arms up to five metres long, but even these have bodies no bigger than an ordinary shopping basket.

Octopuses, squids, and cuttlefishes are all marine animals belonging to the large group known as molluscs. This group also contains the snails, slugs, and bivalves (see page 70). The name mollusc means 'soft', for, although snails and many other molluscs have hard shells, the body itself is always soft. There is no skeleton, and so the molluscs belong to the great division of the animal kingdom known as the invertebrates (see page 8). All the animals described in this book from here onwards are invertebrates.

The octopuses and their relatives are very active molluscs in which the shells are usually very much reduced or even absent. The head end carries two very efficient eyes and contains a brain which is better than that of any other invertebrate animal. The octopuses and squids are certainly the most intelligent of the invertebrates and they learn remarkably quickly. Their most obvious features are the tentacles or arms which spread out from the head end. These are lined with powerful suckers and they are used to catch food. The mouth, right in the centre of the cluster of tentacles, has a very sharp, parrot-like beak. The rest of the body is enveloped in a tough bag of skin called the mantle. There is a large space between the mantle and the body, and it contains the gills. These work just like the gills of a fish (see page 62) to get oxygen from the water. Small openings round the neck allow water to pass into the mantle cavity, and the animal can then squirt out the stale water through a muscular tube called the siphon.

Most of these animals are good at quickly

Above: Two cuttlefishes catching shrimps. The upper animal is shooting out its two long, sucker-covered arms, while the lower one is jetting backwards.

Below: An octopus has caught a crab in its sucker-covered arms. The smaller drawing shows one of the octopus's suckers in more detail.

changing their colours to match different backgrounds. The change is controlled by the nerves and the animals can produce a wide variety of dark and light patterns. When attacked they also have another method of defence. They squirt clouds of black or brown ink out of the siphon and dart away behind these 'smoke' screens.

The octopuses are bottom-living animals that normally stay close to the shore. The body is a rather shapeless sack, with eight arms springing from one end. Large octopuses may occasionally investigate divers with their arms, but they are not aggressive animals. They feed mainly on crabs and other crustaceans and small fishes. By gently pumping water in and out of the mantle cavity, the animals swim jerkily just above the sea bed in their search for food. When a crab is sighted, the octopus turns its siphon backwards and powerfully squirts out water. This sends the octopus forwards and its arms surround and seize the prey. The beak cracks the shell, and a poison is then injected to kill the crab within.

Squids are much more active than octopuses and most of them swim freely at various depths in the oceans. Their bodies are bullet-shaped and, unlike the octopuses, they have slender, horny shells embedded in the mantle. They swim backwards and forwards by jet-propulsion and some shoot into the air like flying fishes. Horizontal fins at the back end help to keep the animals on an even keel. Squids have ten arms, two of which are much longer than the others. These long arms are folded back among the rest when not in use, but they can be shot out at great speed to catch a fish or a prawn. Most squids are only a few centimetres long, but the largest, known as the giant squid, has a body nearly five metres long and its longest arms are about 15 metres long.

Cuttlefishes are broad and flat relatives of the squids. They live on the sea bed and catch shrimps and prawns. They swim rapidly by jet propulsion, but they can also glide gently by waving the edges of the mantle. The cuttlefish has an oval, chalky shell inside its mantle. This shell, or cuttlebone, is often washed up on the beach.

Above: A common squid has fired its smoke screen at a tunny and is now jetting backwards out of harm's way while the fish cannot see it. Below: A cuttlefish showing the position of its 'bone', together with a fossil ammonite – an extinct relative of the squids which had a coiled shell.

Below: One of the squids that live deep down in the sea where it is always dark. Luminous patterns on the animals enable them to find their mates, and the lights also help them to find their way about. The smaller picture shows one of the sharply hooked suckers of the squid.

Above: A typical snail with, on the right, a drawing to show the internal arrangement of its shell and a picture of the radula or tooth ribbon.

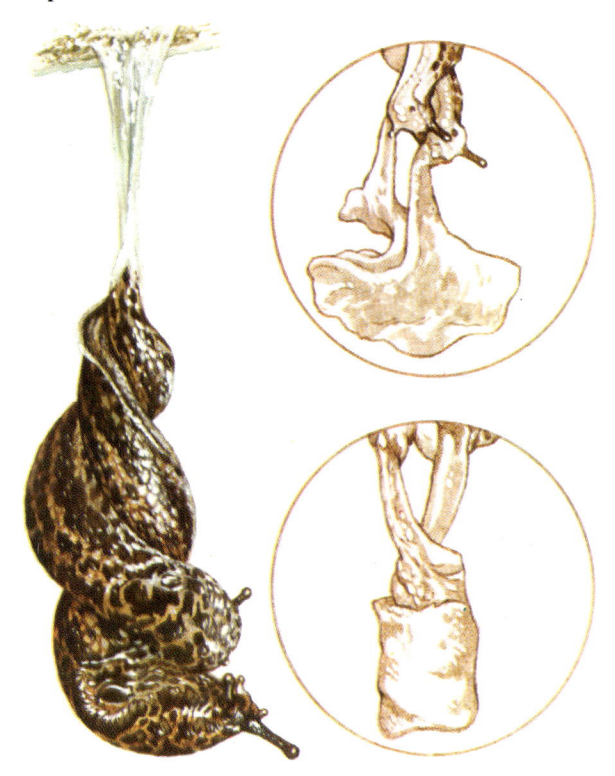

Snails, slugs, and bivalves

The snails and slugs make up the largest group of molluscs. They are called gastropods, a name which means 'belly-foot', because they appear to crawl on their bellies. The gastropods are a very variable and successful group of animals, with members in the sea, on land, and in fresh water.

A snail has a shell which permanently encloses part of its body. The rest of the body can usually be pulled into the shell as well, and there is often a horny lid which is pulled tightly into the opening to protect the snail. This is found especially in aquatic snails. The shell itself is usually coiled, although it may be a simple cone as in the limpets. It is made largely of a form of limestone called calcite, but the outside is covered with horny material which gives the shell its colour. The inside of the shell is coated with a smooth, shiny layer of mother-of-pearl. If a grain of sand gets into the shell and starts to irritate the animal, the skin produces more mother-of-pearl and surrounds the sand with it to produce a pearl. Pearls are more often found in bivalves, however.

The part of the snail's body that is pushed out of the shell is called the foot. Its front end is called the head, although it is not clearly separated from the rest of the foot. The head carries one or two pairs of tentacles. In most land snails the eyes are at the tips of the

Centre: Courting great grey slugs lower themselves on a rope of slime. Twisting round each other in mid air they push out their reproductive organs (circles) and exchange sperm. Each then drops down and lays eggs. Bottom: A mating chain of three sea hares.

The scallop is an unusual bivalve because it can swim about by flapping its two valves.

The tellin buries itself in the sand or mud and uses its siphon to suck up food.

longer tentacles, which are immediately pulled in if the snail bumps into anything. The eyes of water snails are at the base of the tentacles. Glands under the head pour out slime and the animals glide along on this. If you look at the underside of a snail moving over a piece of glass you can see the rippling movements of the muscles which carry it along.

Most land and freshwater snails are plant-eaters, but many sea snails are carnivores. They all have a ribbon-shaped tongue called a radula. It is covered with sharp little teeth like a carpenter's rasp, and the animal uses it to rasp away at its food. The mantle cavity (see page 68) of sea snails and some freshwater snails contains gills for breathing under water, but other freshwater snails and the land snails use their mantle cavity just like a lung. If you watch snails, you can see them opening up the cavity every now and then to take in a fresh supply of air.

Many snails are hermaphrodite, which means that they have both male and female organs in one body. But they still pair up before each goes off to lay eggs. The sea hares, which are halfway between snails and slugs, form pairing chains of several animals, each one fertilizing the one in front.

Slugs, of which there are several distinct groups, are really nothing more than snails without shells. They behave in very similar ways. Many of the sea slugs are beautifully coloured.

Bivalves are molluscs whose shells consist of two halves, or valves, hinged together at one side. These animals include mussels, cockles, oysters, and razor shells. They all live in water and they move about even less than the slugs and snails. Some plough their way slowly through the mud and sand by means of the muscular, tongue-shaped foot, while others never move at all and do not even have a foot. None of them has any head. The mantle (see page 68) forms two tube-like openings called siphons at one end of the body. When the shell opens, one siphon draws water into the body and over the large gills. As well as taking oxygen from the water, the gills trap small food particles which are then wafted along to the mouth. The water then goes out again through the other siphon.

A sea slug eating a sea anemone. The anemone's stinging cells do not hurt the slug, which may even use them for its own protection later.

A tiger cowrie from the South Pacific. Cowries eat sponges, corals, and small sea anemones. The shell has a narrow slit opening at the bottom.

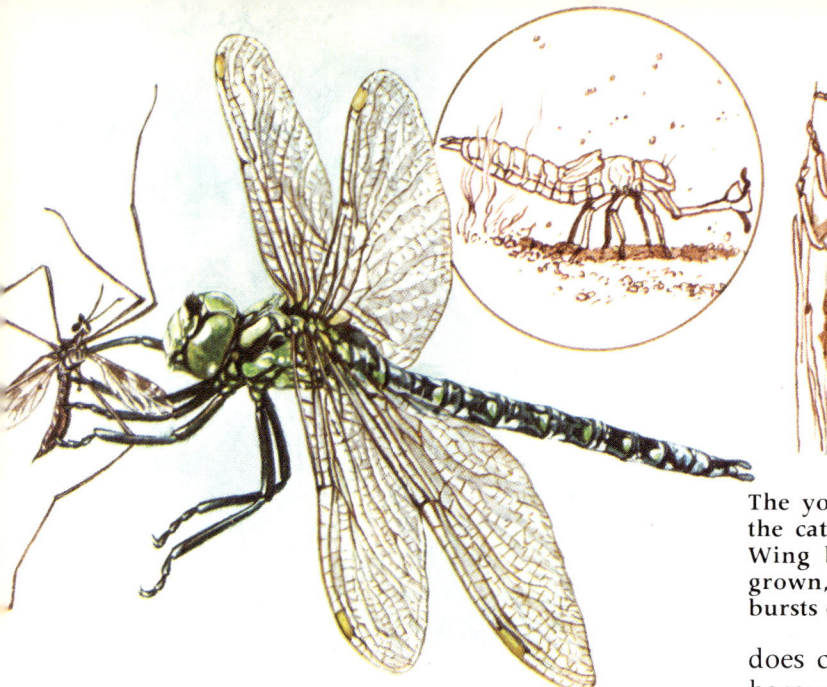

Dragonflies snap up insects in mid air with the aid of their wonderful eyes made up of thousands of tiny lenses (far right), and their spiky legs. The young dragonfly (in circle) shoots out its jaws to catch animals.

Introducing the insects

There are more kinds of insects in the world than there are of all the other animals put together. About a million species have already been discovered, and there must be thousands more still unknown in the forests and other wild places. One of the reasons for their large numbers is that they are all fairly small and can therefore live in many more places than larger animals. Some stick insects have bodies about 30 cm long, and some butterflies and moths span 30 cm across their wings, but these insects all have slender bodies. The bulkiest insect is the goliath beetle from Africa. It is a little bigger than a man's fist and it weighs about 100 grams. At the other end of the scale, there are beetles and other insects smaller than one of the full stops on this page.

The insects belong to the group of animals called arthropods. Crabs, spiders, and centipedes also belong to this group and they all have a tough outer covering on their bodies and their limbs. Like a suit of armour, this covering has a number of flexible joints which allow the animal to move. Although the outer coat provides a good deal of protection, it

The young dragonfly is called a nymph. Unlike the caterpillar, it turns into an adult gradually. Wing buds grow on the body and, when fully grown, the nymph leaves the water and the adult bursts out of its skin (above).

does cause problems for the growing insect, because it cannot grow as the body grows. The young insect therefore has to change its skin every now and then. The old skin splits and the insect wriggles out of it, already wearing a new, loose coat. This new coat is very soft at first, but it soon hardens and gives the insect plenty of room to grow again. The skin-changing process is called moulting and it takes place several times before the insect is fully grown.

An adult insect always has three distinct regions to its body: a head, a thorax, and an abdomen. The head carries a pair of antennae, or feelers, which the insect uses to feel and smell its surroundings. Some male moths have very large antennae with which they can smell the females more than a kilometre away. The thorax, which is the middle region of the body, carries three pairs of legs. It also carries the wings when these are present. Most insects have two pairs of wings, but flies have only one pair and some insects, such as fleas and worker ants, have none at all.

There are very few places on the earth where you will not find insects of some kind or another, although there are not many insects in the sea. You will find them in the soil, inside trees and other plants, inside other animals, in ponds and streams, and sometimes in your food, as well as crawling on the ground and flying about in the air. Most insects stick to a fairly rigid diet of plant or animal material, but between them they make use of just about every edible material in the world. They eat leaves, seeds, flesh, hair,

The pond skater actually skates across the surface of the pond, held up by little pads of water-repellent hairs on its feet. It uses a sharp beak to suck juices from other insects.

Above: An ichneumon fly lays her eggs in the body of a caterpillar. The young ichneumons will feed inside the caterpillar and kill it. Below: A field cricket lays her eggs in the ground.

wood, cork, dung, and blood, and one kind of beetle even eats cigarettes.

Lots of different kinds of jaws are needed to deal with these different foods. The insects' jaws are not inside their mouths like ours are: they are more like tiny legs around the outside of the mouth. Among the dragonflies and grasshoppers these jaws, or mouthparts, are strongly toothed and they are used for biting and chewing solid food. Pond skaters, greenfly and their relatives, all belong to a group of insects called bugs. They all have needle-like mouthparts which fit together to form a minute hypodermic needle. The insects pierce plants or other animals and suck out the juices. Blood-sucking flies have similar mouthparts (see page 77), while butterflies and moths have mouthparts which are more like drinking straws (see page 74).

The carnivorous or flesh-eating insects either go in search of their prey or they lie in wait for it. Some actually set traps. Some caddis larvae, for example, spin silken nets among the water plants and wait for the current to bring them their food. The New Zealand glowworm, which is actually the grub of a fly, lives in caves and hangs lots of sticky threads from the roof. The insect itself glows brightly and the sticky threads sparkle in the light. Other insects are attracted to the light and stick to the threads.

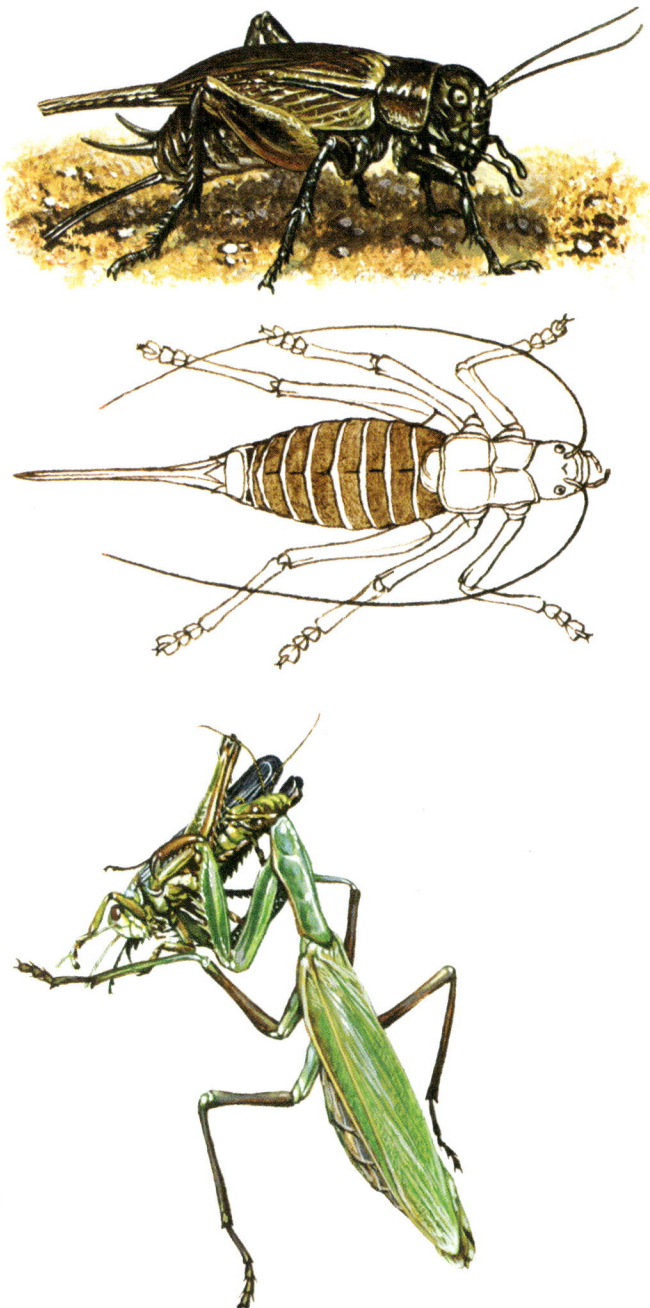

Lower centre: A bush cricket clearly shows the division of the insect body into three regions: head, thorax, and abdomen. Bottom: A praying mantis eating a grasshopper, caught in its spiky front legs.

73

Butterflies and moths

The butterflies and moths belong to a very large group of insects whose wings are covered with tiny scales. These scales give the wings their patterns and colours. If you have held a butterfly's wing in your fingers you will know how easily the scales rub off.

Moths are far more numerous than butterflies, although we see more butterflies because they fly in the daytime. Most moths fly at night, but there are some very brightly coloured day-flying moths as well. The best way to separate butterflies from moths is to look at the antennae: the tips are always swollen in butterflies and they often look like slender pins. Very few moths have antennae like this, and those that do never close their wings together above the body like the butterflies. Several butterflies and moths, including the magnificent birdwing butterflies of the New Guinea region, measure 30 cm across their wings. At the lower end of the scale, the smallest butterfly is the South African dwarf blue, which has a wingspan of about 14 mm. Among the moths however there are several that measure no more than 4 mm across their wings. These insects are so small that they spend their early lives tunnelling between the upper and lower surfaces of leaves.

Apart from a few very small moths which chew pollen, the butterflies and moths are liquid feeders. Their mouthparts form a slender tube called a proboscis or tongue. It is coiled up under the head when not in use, but when the insect smells something sweet, such as the nectar of a flower, the proboscis is uncoiled and used to suck up the liquid like a straw. Most butterflies and moths feed on nectar, but some also like the juices of ripe fruit and rotting meat and they often gather to drink from puddles. One Malayan moth has taken to a diet of blood. The tip of its proboscis is very sharp and it can pierce the skin of a buffalo to suck out some blood. As we shall see later, the diets of young butterflies and moths are very different from those of the adults.

After mating, the female lays her eggs and leaves them. They hatch in about two weeks, but the insects that come out do not look anything like butterflies. They are caterpillars, and instead of tubular mouthparts they have biting jaws. They start eating right away. By 'tasting' the leaves with sensitive pads on her feet the butterfly usually makes sure that she lays her eggs on the right kind of plant for the caterpillars. Most caterpillars feed on leaves, but some eat seeds and fruit and some even chew through wood. The caterpillars of clothes-moths prefer wool and are among the few caterpillars that eat animal material.

The silkworm caterpillar using its strong jaws to munch mulberry leaves. Another caterpillar (in circle), spinning its silken cocoon.

A hawkmoth using its enormously long tongue to drink nectar from a flower. The moth is hovering while it drinks.

Right: A much enlarged drawing of the scales on a butterfly's wing.

Caterpillars and other young insects that look nothing like their parents are called larvae. They grow quite rapidly and change their skins four or five times. They are then ready for the next stage in their lives, which is called the pupa or chrysalis. Most butterfly caterpillars hang upside down when they are about to change into pupae, or else they secure themselves to plant stems with silken belts. Many moth caterpillars make themselves snug chambers in the soil, while others, among the leaves and twigs, spin silken cocoons around themselves. A completed cocoon has many metres of silk thread, all produced from the caterpillar's body.

When preparations are complete the caterpillar's skin splits yet again, but this time a shiny chrysalis appears instead of another caterpillar skin. The chrysalis does not feed or move about, but there is great activity inside it because this is where the caterpillar's body is converted into that of the adult. The rebuilding may take only a few days in the summer, and then the adult breaks out of the chrysalis skin. Its wings are soft and crumpled at first, so the insect hangs itself up to dry. Its wings soon fill out and harden and the butterfly or moth is then ready to fly away.

The caterpillar of the puss moth, puffing up its head end and waving its 'tails' to make itself look fierce and frighten away an enemy.

Below: The life cycle of the red admiral butterfly.
1. Egg; 2. Young caterpillar emerging from egg; 3. Adult caterpillar changing into chrysalis; 4. Chrysalis; 5. Butterfly emerging from chrysalis; 6. Adult butterfly.

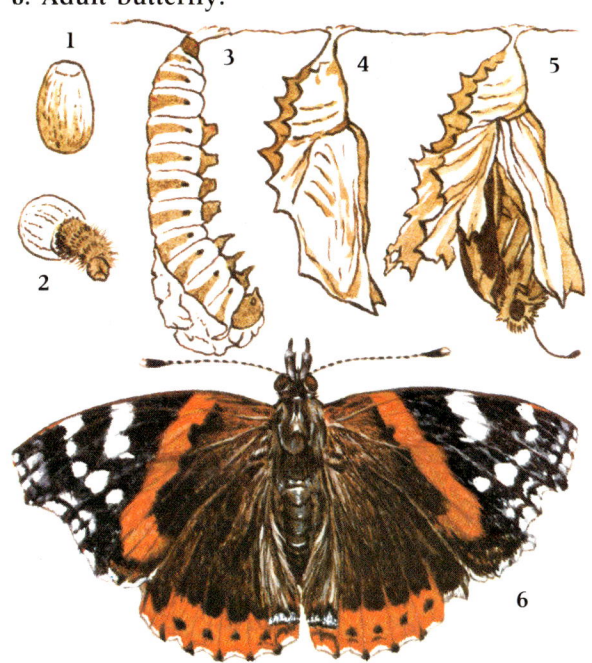

Below: The garden tiger moth, displaying its brightly coloured wings which warn birds and other animals that the insect is not nice to eat.

Beetles and flies

The two groups of insects seen on this page both have life histories like the butterflies and moths, because they all go through a chrysalis or pupal stage. Anatomically, however, they are very different from each other.

Beetles generally have two pairs of wings, but the front pair are hard and horny. They are called elytra and they protect the delicate flying wings that are folded up beneath them. The tough elytra allow beetles to live in the soil, where more delicate winged insects could not exist. They also enable the insects to live in water because the space between them and the body acts as a reservoir of air. Water beetles, whose legs are usually broad and paddle-like, can stay under the water for long periods, but they have to come to the surface every now and then to renew the air in their reservoirs.

The beetles all have sharp, biting jaws and they use them to eat all kinds of solid food, both plant and animal. Adults and larvae usually eat the same kind of food. Many of the beetles are pests because they damage our own food and materials. Examples include the Colorado beetle which eats potato leaves, the furniture beetle or woodworm which destroys our timber, and the grain weevil. The latter lives in grain stores and destroys huge amounts of wheat and other cereals. On the other hand, there are many useful beetles, such as the ladybirds which eat the harmful greenfly in our gardens. Many beetles are also important scavengers, burying and eating animal dung and carcasses. Some dung beetles actually roll balls of dung about until they find a suitable place to bury them. The young are reared on the buried dung.

Among the many other well known beetles are the fireflies and the true glow-worms. These insects have light-producing organs which attract their mates.

Flies

The flies have only one pair of wings, but just behind the wings there is a pair of pin-shaped objects called balancers. They are easily seen in the daddy-long-legs, or cranefly. They help the insects to keep their balance during flight and they are thought to be the greatly altered hind wings.

Flies are all liquid feeders, their food ranging from nectar to dung and the blood of other animals. Several different kinds of mouthparts are needed to deal with these different diets. Fly larvae are always legless and they usually eat quite different materials from the adults. Many fly species are serious pests, some of them doing the damage as adults and some as larvae.

The common house-fly is one of the most dangerous pests because of its filthy habits. It breeds in dung and other decaying material, and the adults feed on the germ-laden fluids around these materials. Covered with germs, they then often come to our meal tables and walk on our food. Although they usually just soak up liquids with their mop-like mouthparts, they can also dissolve solid food by pouring saliva on to it and then soaking up the solution.

Below: A pair of burying beetles with a dead mouse.

Above: A scarab dung beetle rolling a ball of dung by pushing it with its back legs.

A Colorado beetle (left) and its larva on potato.

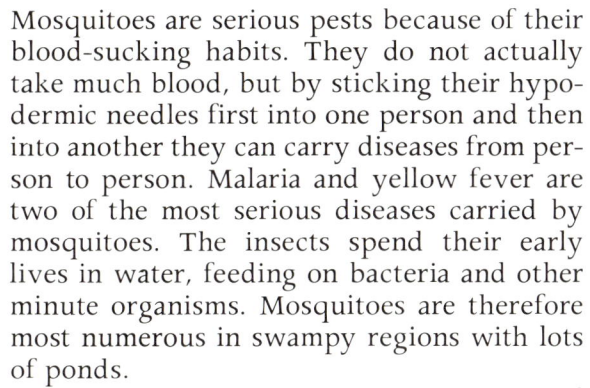

A two-spot ladybird eating an aphid (greenfly).

Mosquitoes are serious pests because of their blood-sucking habits. They do not actually take much blood, but by sticking their hypodermic needles first into one person and then into another they can carry diseases from person to person. Malaria and yellow fever are two of the most serious diseases carried by mosquitoes. The insects spend their early lives in water, feeding on bacteria and other minute organisms. Mosquitoes are therefore most numerous in swampy regions with lots of ponds.

Among the flies which are pests in the larval stage are the crane-flies and the warble-flies. Crane-fly grubs are known as leather-jackets and they nibble the roots of cereals and other plants. Warble-fly grubs live in the bodies of cattle and produce nasty sores when they eat their way out through the skin.

Below: A common gnat or mosquito plunging its beak into human skin to suck blood. The insect in the circle is the larva of the mosquito which lives in water.

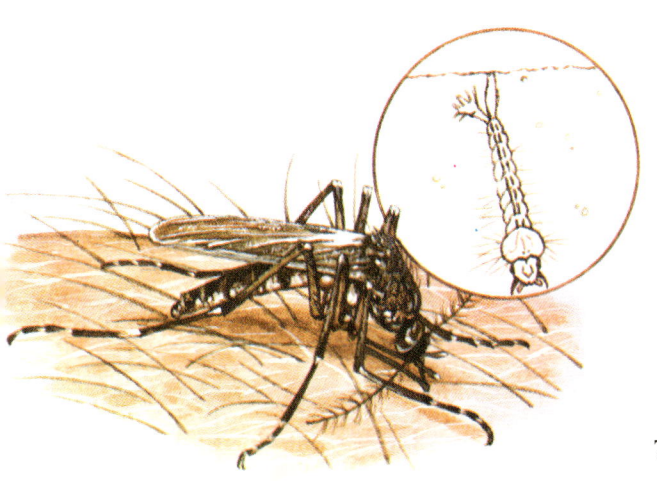

Above: A large robber-fly carrying off a smaller fly to eat.

Left: bee-fly

Below: A crane-fly, or daddy-long-legs

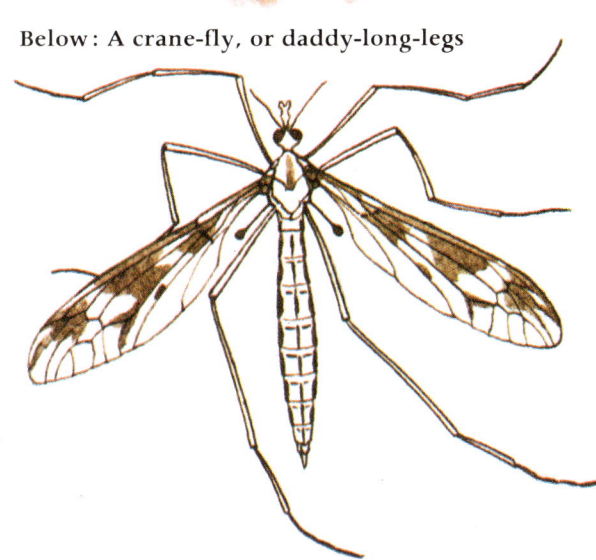

Above: Hornets leaving their delicate paper nest. Circle inset: Cells in tiers within the nest. Below left: Part of honey bee comb showing the six-sided wax cells, some with grubs. Below right: Pollen baskets on hind legs, (left) empty pollen basket, (right) full basket.

The social insects

In the middle of the summer a common wasp nest may contain about 4,000 wasps at various stages of life. All are the children of one wasp – the queen – who started the nest in the spring, and they all work together for the good of the family as a whole. This is what is meant by social insects. Chemicals produced by the queen are spread through the whole community and they control the activity of the other wasps and ensure that things run smoothly. Almost all the wasps in the colony are small females called workers. Some of them collect wood pulp to make the nest, others collect food, while yet others stay at home and do the housework and feed the young wasps. When once she has started the nest and reared a few workers, the queen does little but lay eggs.

Towards the end of the summer some male wasps are reared, together with some large females which will become queens. No more eggs are laid in the nest after this and the workers, with no more grubs to feed, turn their attention to our fruit and jam. The males and young queens mate, but only the new queens survive the autumn cold. They find cosy places for their winter sleep and in spring start new nests.

Bumble bees have similar life histories to the wasps, although they feed their grubs on nectar and pollen instead of the chewed insects which wasps give to their youngsters. Bumble bee colonies are also smaller than wasp colonies, with only a few hundred bees at the most.

The honey bee is a very different insect, and its colonies go on for many years. Each colony is ruled by a queen, but she is unable to do anything apart from lay eggs. During her lifetime she may lay well over half a million eggs. She is always surrounded by worker bees who feed her and clean her. While doing this they pick up the 'queen substance' which controls their behaviour. This also happens in the wasp colony.

Left: A bumble bee tending to the round wax chambers in which she has laid her eggs. The nest is on or under the ground.

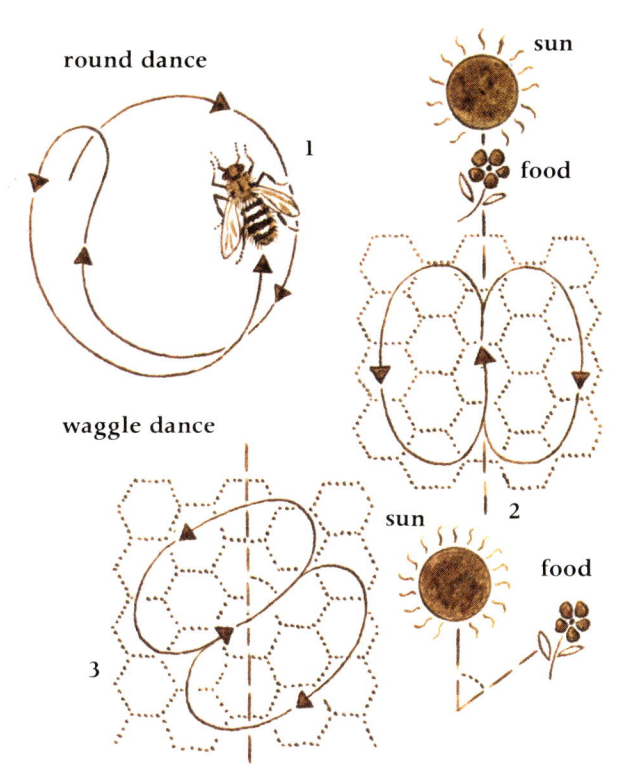

When food is near the honey bee does the round dance (1), and the waggle dance (2) when food is farther away. The angle of the dance on the comb is the same as the angle between sun and food, so the bees know where to go.

Honey bees make wax in their bodies and use it to build the neat six-sided cells which make up the nest. The cells are used as store rooms for pollen and honey, and the young bees are also reared in them. Worker bees will fly several kilometres in search of food, and when they have found a good supply they go back to the nest or hive and tell their sisters about it. They do this by dancing on the honeycombs. The speed and direction of the dances tell the other workers the distance and direction of the food. These other bees can then fly straight to the flowers instead of wasting time looking for them and they can collect the maximum amount of food. On returning to the hive, they give up their pollen and nectar to the 'house-maid' bees who convert the nectar into honey and put it into the cells.

At any one time there may be about 50,000 workers in the colony, and during the summer months there are usually a few males or drones. If numbers increase too much and the colony becomes overcrowded the workers make some special large cells and rear some new queens in them by giving the grubs special food. The old queen then flies away with a swarm of workers to start a new nest, and one of the new queens takes over the old colony. She makes her marriage flight and mates with some drones and then settles down to a life of egg-laying.

The ants resemble the honey bees in that their colonies go on for many years, but their way of life is very different. The workers are all wingless and they are often of several different types. Large-headed types are called soldiers and they defend the colony with their huge jaws. Winged ants appear only during the mating season, when swarms of males and young queens appear. The queens break off their wings after mating.

The other great group of social insects are the termites. They are like ants in many ways, but each colony is ruled by a king and queen instead of just by a queen.

Below: Weaver ants fixing leaves together to make the nest. Bottom: African termites and their huge nest, with a drawing showing what it is like inside. The nests may be more than 6 metres high.

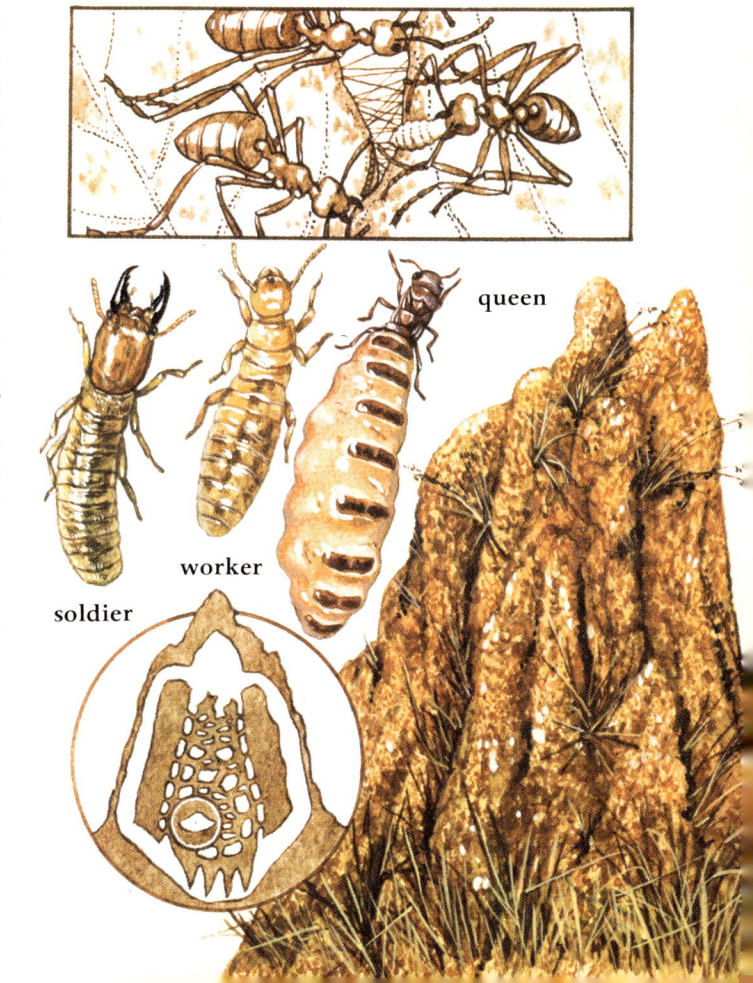

Left: An orb-web spider carefully positioning the threads of her web with her back legs. Below left: The curious purse-web spider lives inside a closed tube and grabs insects through the silk.

Spiders and scorpions

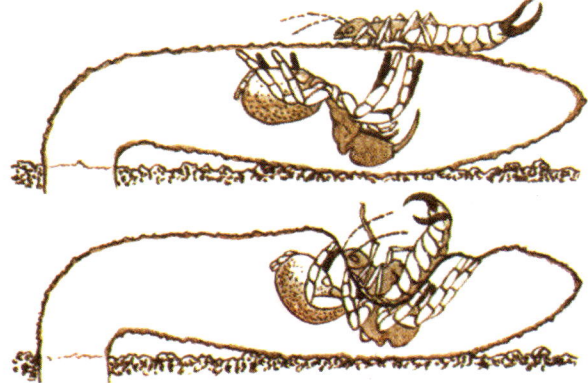

Spiders and scorpions, like insects, are members of the vast animal group called arthropods. They differ from insects, however, in never having wings or antennae and in having four pairs of legs instead of three. They are not closely related to the insects and they are known as arachnids.

There are well over 20,000 different kinds of spiders in the world. Very few of them live in water, but they are everywhere on land and they exist in enormous numbers. It has been calculated that one hectare (about 2·5 acres) of grassland may support more than five million spiders in the summer. Imagine how many more flies and midges there would be to annoy us if the spiders were not there to catch them.

The largest spiders are the bird-eating spiders of tropical areas. They are very hairy and some have legs spanning 25 cm., although their bodies are only about nine centimetres long. They eat young birds and other animals, but they are not particularly dangerous to people. Their bite is very painful, but their poison is less dangerous than that of the much smaller black widow spiders. Bird-eating spiders are often called tarantulas, but this is wrong: the tarantulas are large wolf spiders living in southern Europe.

The best known spiders are those that make the beautiful round orb webs on our plants and fences. They include the plump brown garden spider and, in warmer lands, many colourful species. The web is not actually a home for the spider, but a deadly trap for flies and other insects. It is made of fine silk, which the spider makes in its own body, and coated with droplets of gum. The orb web is only one of many kinds of webs. Other well-known types include the lace-like webs that spread out from holes in walls, and the hammock webs spun in the grass by the little money spiders. Silk threads stretch like scaffolding above the hammocks, and when an insect blunders into them it falls on to the hammock to be snapped up. The purse-web spider lives in a closed silken tube which is partly buried in the ground. When an insect walks over the upper part of the tube the spider rushes up and spears it with its fangs. The insect is then pulled into the tube and the spider sucks it dry. Arachnids do not have proper jaws and they can only suck up crushed or liquefied food.

Not all spiders make webs. The trap-door spider hides in a burrow and grabs passing insects. Crab spiders are often brightly coloured and sit unnoticed in flowers just waiting for an insect to come along. Wolf spiders and jumping spiders go out to hunt. Jumping spiders have huge eyes and they pounce on their prey with amazing accuracy. The spitting spider actually fires a network of sticky threads over its prey to trap it.

All spiders make and use silk, even if they do not make webs. The eggs are always wrapped in silken cocoons, and many spiders pay out silk life-lines when they fall. They

The trap-door spider resting in its burrow.

A tropical bird-eating spider about to have dinner.

climb up again later and usually eat the silk as they go. The water spider actually makes a home with silk. It makes a thimble-shaped net under water and fills it with air bubbles so that it can live there.

Scorpions are basically ground-living arachnids and they are easily recognized by the large claws at the front and the slender tail which curves round over the body and ends in a sting. The animals are found mainly in the tropical regions, especially in dry areas, and some are very dangerous because of their stings. They usually eat insects and other small animals which they catch with their claws. The sting is not often used to kill the prey. A pair of very small tweezer-like organs by the mouth help to tear and crush the food before it is swallowed. Scorpions perform elaborate courtship dances, and the females then give birth to active young. The babies are carried around on their mother's back for the first few days of their lives.

A scorpion carrying its youngsters on its back has just caught a lizard with its large claws.

Right: The tarantula, a hunting spider from southern Europe. Below right: A harvestman, clearly showing its one-piece body, which separates it from the spiders. Below: A false scorpion, very highly magnified.

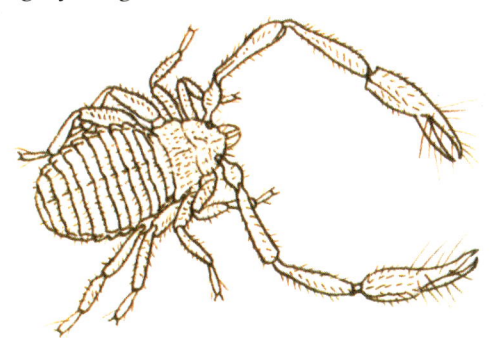

Crabs and lobsters

The crabs and lobsters form yet another division of the great group of animals called arthropods. They are known as crustaceans because their bodies are largely covered by a hard, crust-like coat. This is made of a horny material combined with lime to make it hard. Flexible joints allow the animals to move. Like the insects and other arthropods, the crustaceans have to change their skins as they grow. Crustaceans have several or many pairs of legs, one or more of which often end in prominent pincers. The animals almost all live in water. They breathe by means of gills which are attached to or even formed by some of the legs.

Crabs are marine crustaceans whose bodies are generally rather flat and broad. The abdomen is small and usually hidden away under the rest of the body. The animals lift themselves up on the tips of their legs and walk over the sea bed or the shore with a strange sideways movement. Some species have rather broad, hairy legs which they use as paddles for swimming. Male fiddler crabs have one claw very much larger than the other. They sit on the sand and wave the large claw up and down to attract the females for mating. Hermit crabs are more slender creatures with a soft abdomen which is not curved under the body. The crabs find empty sea shells to live in, thus protecting their soft hind quarters. They have to find new shells every now and then to house their growing bodies.

Most crabs are scavenging animals, using their pincers to pick up anything edible from the sand or mud. The pincers work very rapidly, often picking up several sand grains every second and holding them to the mouth for feathery mouth parts to sweep in anything edible. Larger food particles are torn to pieces by the largest pincers. The robber crab, which is a large relative of the hermit crab, lives on land and even climbs trees. It eats almost anything and is particularly fond of fallen coconuts which it finds on the sea shore. Lobsters and their relatives are much more elongated and less flattened than the crabs. The common lobster, which may reach a weight of five kilograms, lives on the sea bed and feeds on living and dead animals. It normally walks, but it can swim by waving

Top left: A robber crab eating a fallen coconut. Above: A hermit crab in a whelk shell. Below: A male fiddler crab waving its one enormous claw.

the small, paddle-like limbs on its abdomen. The freshwater crayfish leads a similar life in clear streams. Prawns and shrimps are smaller relatives of the lobsters and crayfish. Some live on the sea bed, while others swim freely in the sea, often at great depths. The females carry their eggs about, attached to the swimming limbs under the abdomen. At these times the animals are said to be 'in berry', because the eggs are just like hundreds of tiny berries.

Barnacles are marine crustaceans that spend their adult lives attached to rocks and other objects. They can close their shells when the tide goes out, but when the water returns they open up and 'comb' food from it with their delicate spiky legs. Young barnacles look nothing like the adults and they spend their lives drifting in the surface layers of the sea. Young crabs and lobsters are also very different from the adults, and they drift in the plankton as well.

Many adult crustaceans are small planktonic

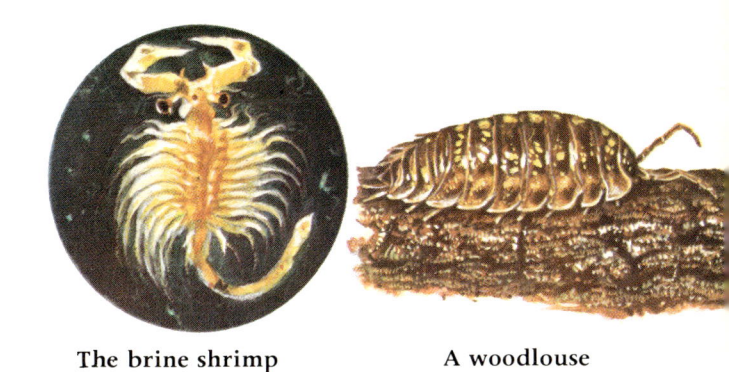

The brine shrimp   A woodlouse

Above: The acorn barnacle (left) and the goose barnacle, two crustaceans which in the adult state remain fixed to rocks and other objects.

The freshwater crayfish or white-claw.

creatures, found in both salt and fresh water. The brine shrimp lives in salty pools and swims on its back by waving rows of delicate limbs. At the same time, these limbs absorb oxygen and filter food from the water. Small ponds often contain thousands of tiny pink animals that bob up and down in the surface layers. These are water fleas – little crustaceans that swim jerkily along by 'rowing' with their large antennae. Smaller limbs, partly enclosed in a cloak-like shell, filter food particles from the water.

The only group of crustaceans which live permanently on land are the woodlice or sow-bugs, but even these are confined to relatively damp places because they still breathe largely with gills. The gills are very thin, leaf-like objects on the underside of the abdomen. As long as their surfaces are kept moist, the animals can absorb oxygen efficiently. Woodlice are all oval and generally rather flattened animals and most of them are less than two centimetres long. They feed mainly on decaying plants, although some species eat growing seedlings. They hide under logs and stones during the daytime and come out at night when the air is damp. Several species live on the sea shore.

The Japanese spider crab, largest of all crustaceans.

Starfishes, urchins, and sea anemones

Starfishes and sea urchins belong to a large group or phylum of animals called echinoderms. This name means 'spiny skins', and if you examine one of the animals next time you go to the seaside you will see that it is a very good name. Chalky plates embedded in the skin make the animals very rough to touch. The echinoderms all live in the sea and they are all built on a circular plan.

The starfishes all have a number of arms spreading out from a central disc. The mouth is on the underside, and the undersides of the arms carry numerous little tubes known as tube feet. Each tube normally ends in a sucker. The animal can extend the tube feet by pumping water into them, and by fixing the suckers to stones on the sea bed it can drag itself along. The tube feet are also used for opening cockles and other bivalves. Suckers are fixed to both valves of the shell and they hold so tightly that the starfish can drag the valves apart. It then pushes part of its stomach out through its mouth and digests the unfortunate mollusc. In addition to their use in moving and feeding, the tube feet absorb a lot of the animal's oxygen requirements from the water.

The chalky plates of a sea urchin's skin are all joined together to form a complete shell called a test. It is covered with skin in the living animal, but hollow, naked shells are

A starfish opening a mussel with its tube feet.

often washed up on the beach. Each shell has five rows or arms of tiny holes showing where the tube feet passed through. Little round knobs show where the animal's spines were attached. The sea urchin's mouth is on the underside and it is provided with a complex system of rods known as Aristotle's lantern. The rods form a pointed beak with which the urchin rasps small plants and animals from the sea bed. The tube feet on the lower surface have suckers and are used for movement, but those further up have no suckers. They help to absorb oxygen, and many also act as sense organs to detect vibrations in the water. Like the other echinoderms, the sea urchins never mate. The females scatter their eggs in the water and the males discharge their sperm. Some eggs get fertilized in the water and grow into new animals.

Other echinoderms include the brittle stars,

The violet sea urchin grazes on seaweeds. The heart urchin has very short spines and it burrows in the sand where it eats decaying matter.

The sea anemone on the left has caught a small fish. The one on the right is out of the water and closed right up to prevent itself from drying up.

heart urchin shell

violet sea urchin

The Portuguese man-o'-war has caught a fish.

The common jelly fish *(Aurelia)* **is harmless.**

which have much thinner arms than the starfishes, the sea lilies, and the sea cucumbers. The latter are cucumber-shaped and they have some very large tube feet round the mouth at one end. These tube feet sweep food particles into the mouth.

The sea anemones belong to a much simpler group of animals called coelenterates. Each is little more than a hollow bag with a ring of tentacles round the mouth. Sea anemones, which look more like flowers than animals, attach themselves to underwater rocks and spread their tentacles to wait for dinner to arrive. They feed on fishes, shrimps, and other small animals which come within reach of the tentacles. Each tentacle is covered with stinging cells just like those of the freshwater *Hydra* (see page 88). Their prey is paralyzed by the stings and the tentacles then push it into the anemone's mouth. When the tide goes out the anemones pull in their tentacles and close up to look like little blobs of jelly.

Corals are like miniature sea anemones that surround themselves with little limestone cups. Many of the animals branch repeatedly like miniature trees, and their cups build up branching skeletons of various shapes. These skeletons form the coral reefs of the tropical seas.

The other main group of coelenterates are the jellyfishes, most of which float at the surface of the sea with their mouths on the underside. Some suck in tiny animals, but others catch fishes with their stinging tentacles. The Portuguese man-o'-war is not a true jellyfish. It is more like a colony of hydra-like animals hanging from a gas-filled float. Chains of tentacles hang down into the water to catch unwary fishes. The poison in the tentacles is strong enough to be dangerous to people.

The gorgonian corals have rather horny skeletons and they are softer than the true corals, but very attractive.

Coral colonies build up when the animals produce branches (right), but the animals can also scatter eggs into the water (left).

common earthworm

The world of worms

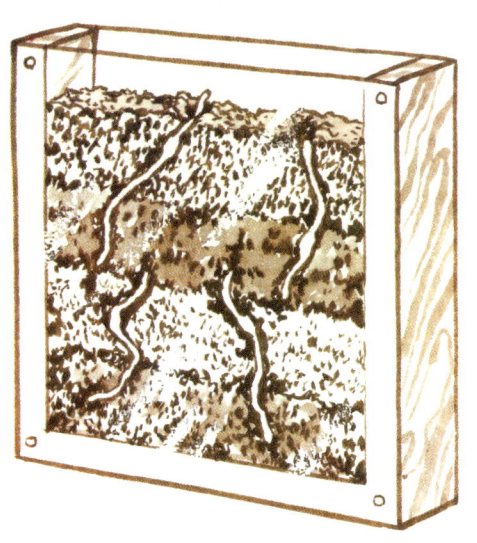

You can watch earthworms ploughing through the soil by making a simple glass-sided cage (above) and filling it with soil. Keep it in the dark.

Many slender, legless animals are called worms, but they belong to several very different groups. Tapeworms, which live as parasites inside the bodies of other animals, are like lengths of ribbon. They belong to a group called flatworms. Many round worms or nematodes also live inside other animals, but they can be distinguished from tapeworms because they look like pieces of plastic-coated wire.

The largest group of worms are the annelids, whose bodies are clearly divided into a number of rings or segments. Members of this group include the earthworms, the leeches, and numerous marine animals called bristleworms.

The earthworms that tunnel through the soil range from tiny potworms only a few millimetres long to tropical giants of more than three metres. The typical worms that we dig up in our gardens are generally a few centimetres long and most are pinkish brown in colour. They exist in enormous numbers – perhaps a million worms under the grass of a normal football pitch – and they play a very important role in keeping the soil in good condition.

The earthworm has no obvious head and no eyes or ears, but there is a definite front end with a simple brain. This end is more pointed than the hind end. The number of segments varies from species to species, but a typical earthworm has about 150 segments. They are all more or less alike, except for five or six segments about a quarter the way along from the front. These segments are somewhat swollen and they form the saddle. They are concerned with egg-laying. Each body segment has four pairs of small bristles which help it to move along. They dig into the soil and hold one part of the body firm while another part is pushed or pulled along.

The worm feeds on decaying plant matter, which it gets by swallowing soil. The unwanted soil particles pass out of the hind end as worm casts at or just under the surface. The worms thus act as valuable ploughs, bringing mineral-rich soil up to the surface for plants to use. Their tunnels also help to ventilate and drain the soil.

Earthworms are hermaphrodite animals, with both male and female organs in one animal, but they still pair up before laying eggs. After mating, each animal's saddle produces

The medicinal leech was once used to suck 'bad blood' from people who were ill.

Spirographis is a bristleworm living in a thin tube on the sea bed. Its numerous tentacles filter food from the water.

The lugworm tunnels in the mud and throws up piles of worm casts. Fishermen dig up this worm and use it as bait.

a collar which slides off over the front end and takes some eggs with it. The collar forms a little cocoon around the eggs.

Leeches are mainly water-living worms, although some species can be found in moist soil. They are easily recognized by their large suckers and their ability to contract rapidly from a thin ribbon to a rounded blob. Leeches are famous for their blood-sucking habits, but they are not all blood-suckers. Most of them actually feed on water snails and other small animals. Horny teeth cut up the food, or merely cut the skin for the blood-sucking leeches to get to work. Leeches are hermaphrodite and produce egg cocoons in the same way as the earthworms.

The bristleworms get their name because most of the body segments carry tufts of bristles. They all live in the sea, but they have many very different ways of life. The ragworms are free-swimming animals with horny jaws. Some eat other animals, and some browse on seaweeds. Lugworms tunnel in the mud or sand like earthworms, while many other bristleworms make tubes in which to live. The tubes may be composed of sand grains which the worms pick up and stick together, or of limestone which the animal secretes. Tentacles round the mouths of these worms are used for collecting food. Some sweep sand and other material into the mouth for sifting, while others filter small particles from the water and pass them along to the mouth.

Serpula (above) makes limestone tubes in which to live. It can close its tube with a plug when not feeding. The animal below, without any rings, is a flatworm – quite a different kind of animal.

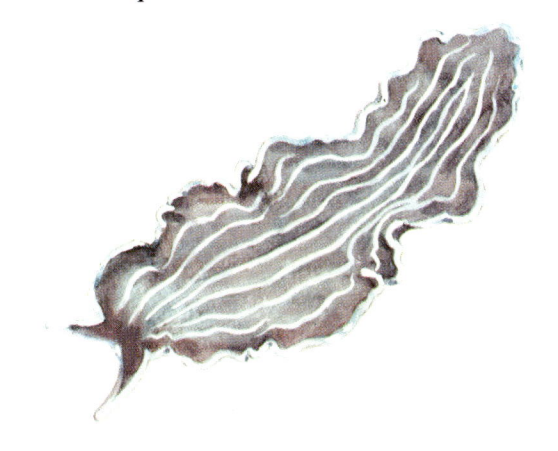

87

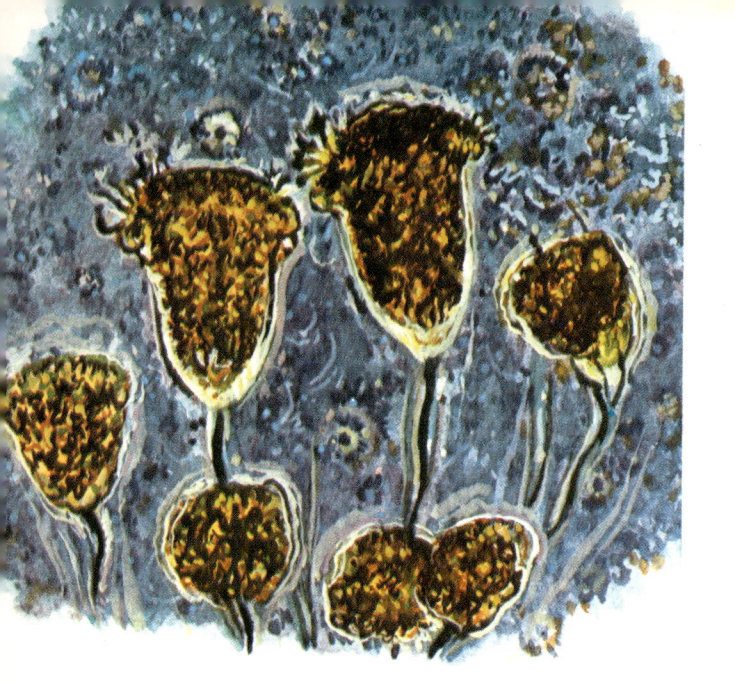

Nature in miniature

If you dip a jam jar into a pond and look carefully at the water you collect you will undoubtedly see lots of things moving around in it. Water fleas and other small crustaceans (see page 83) may well be bobbing up and down in the water, and you will probably see some young mosquitoes (see page 77). There may also be some water mites gliding smoothly about in your jar. These are tiny relatives of the spiders, with bodies like little round pinheads. If you collect some water weeds in your jar you might be lucky enough to see a fascinating creature called hydra hanging from the leaves.

Hydra is like a very slender sea anemone, dangling a number of slender arms in the water. It looks quite harmless and is harmless to us, but it is a death trap for a water flea that blunders into its arms. The arms, like those of the sea anemones, are covered with minute stinging cells which are rather like miniature harpoons. As soon as the water flea touches an arm the harpoons are fired and the victim is trapped. Some of the harpoons have sharp points and they stick into the victim and inject poison, but others are simply whip-like threads which coil round the legs of the victim and hold it firmly. The arms then bend round and push the victim into hydra's mouth.

You will sometimes see a hydra with two or three sets of arms branching from one main body. This is how the animal reproduces itself when the water is reasonably warm. Buds appear on the sides of the body and they develop their own mouths and tentacles. Eventually, each branch breaks away and becomes a separate animal. In the autumn hydra produces a few thick-walled eggs which survive the winter and grow into new animals in the spring.

You can just about watch hydra at work with your naked eye, although it is only a few millimetres long and you will not be

Vorticella (above), also known as the bell animalcule (little animal), forms little colonies on water plants. Tiny cilia waft food particles into the mouth.

Below: Some common protozoans. The radiolarian lives in the sea, but the others are found in fresh water. The heliozoan rolls along on its arms.

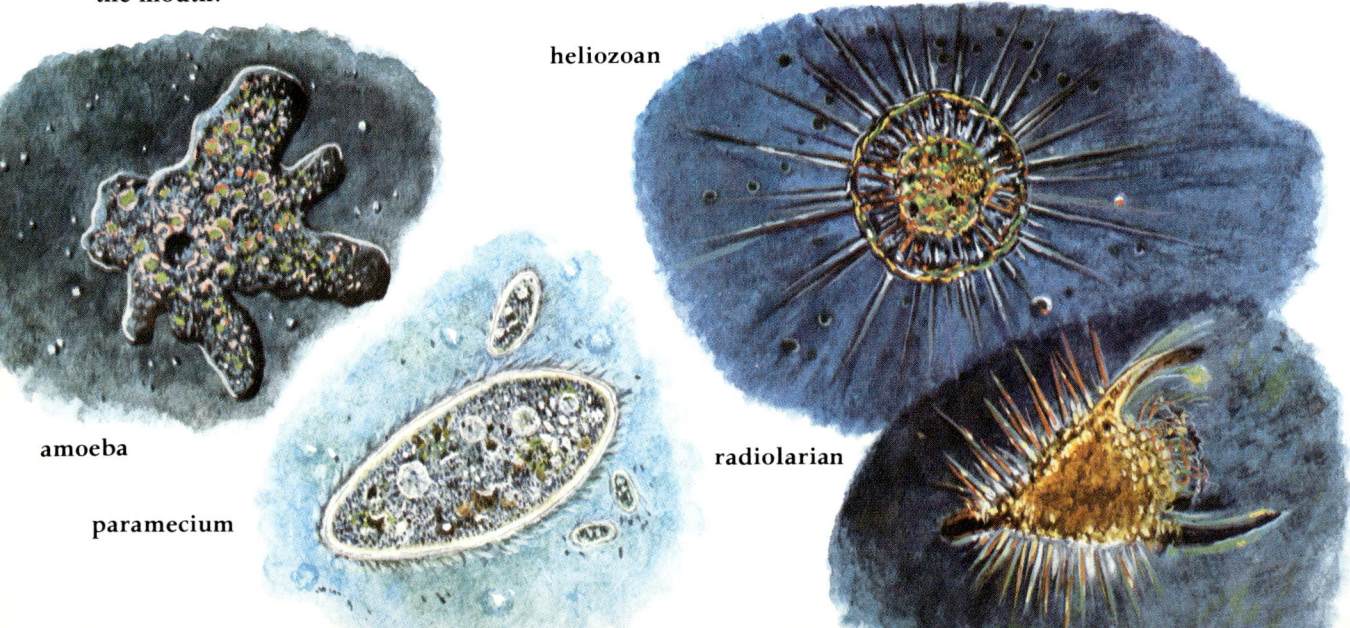

amoeba

paramecium

heliozoan

radiolarian

Right: Stentor is a funnel-shaped protozoan up to about a millimetre long. It fixes itself to water plants and sucks in other tiny animals.

able to see the harpoons, but there are many more animals in the water that are too small for you to see without a microscope. Most of these animals are called protozoans. Their bodies consist of just one tiny cell, in contrast to the countless millions of cells that make up our own bodies. But all the seven life processes described on page 8 go on in this one cell. The processes are all controlled by a denser part of the cell – the nucleus. This represents the 'brain' of the protozoan.

One of the commonest protozoans in the pond is known as amoeba. It is like a little speck of jelly with an elastic skin, and it is continually changing shape as it puts out 'arms' in various directions and flows first this way and then that. It 'swallows' bacteria and other microscopic food particles by simply flowing around them. Digestive juices then dissolve the food and the amoeba absorbs the digested material. Any undissolved material is left behind as the animal flows away from it. As with most very small water-living animals, there are no special breathing organs. The animal can absorb enough oxygen from the water through the body's surface.

As it goes on feeding and growing, amoeba reaches a size at which it appears to be too big for its nucleus. A very strange thing then happens: the nucleus splits into two and then the whole body breaks into two parts. Each part takes half of the original nucleus and goes on living in the normal way as a new amoeba. These new creatures will also divide when they are big enough, and so amoeba is theoretically immortal: it goes on living for ever unless, as happens to the majority of individuals, it gets eaten. If the pond gets cold or dries up, the amoeba can form a tough coat around itself. Inside the coat, it can divide into dozens of small individuals which escape when conditions improve.

Paramecium is another common pond-living protozoan. It is clothed with minute hairs called cilia. It swims by waving the cilia to and fro. Food particles are also wafted into the mouth by the beating cilia.

Centre below: Hydra has caught a water flea and is pushing it into its mouth with its tentacles.

Bottom: Hundreds of stinging cells occur along the hydra's arms. The 'harpoons' are neatly coiled inside their cells to start with, and they are fired when the trigger hairs are touched. Discharged cells cannot be used again, but hydra is always making new cells to replace them.

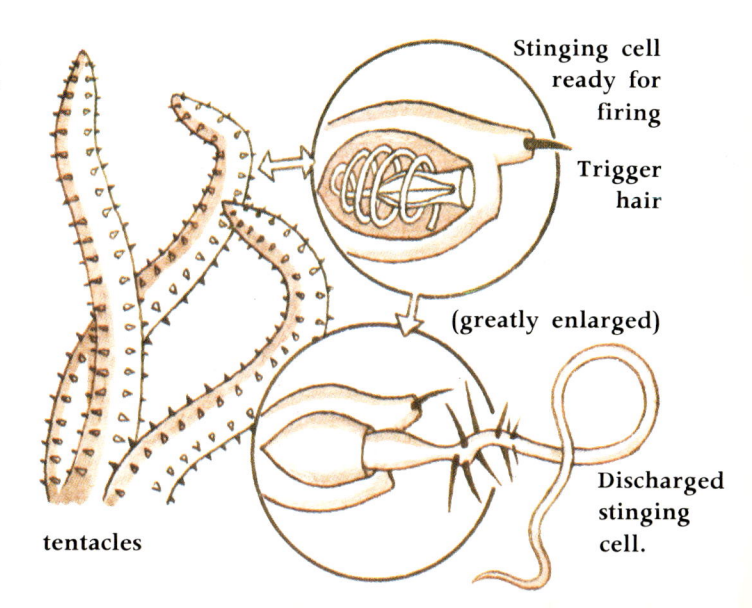

Stinging cell ready for firing

Trigger hair

(greatly enlarged)

Discharged stinging cell.

tentacles

The tree of evolution

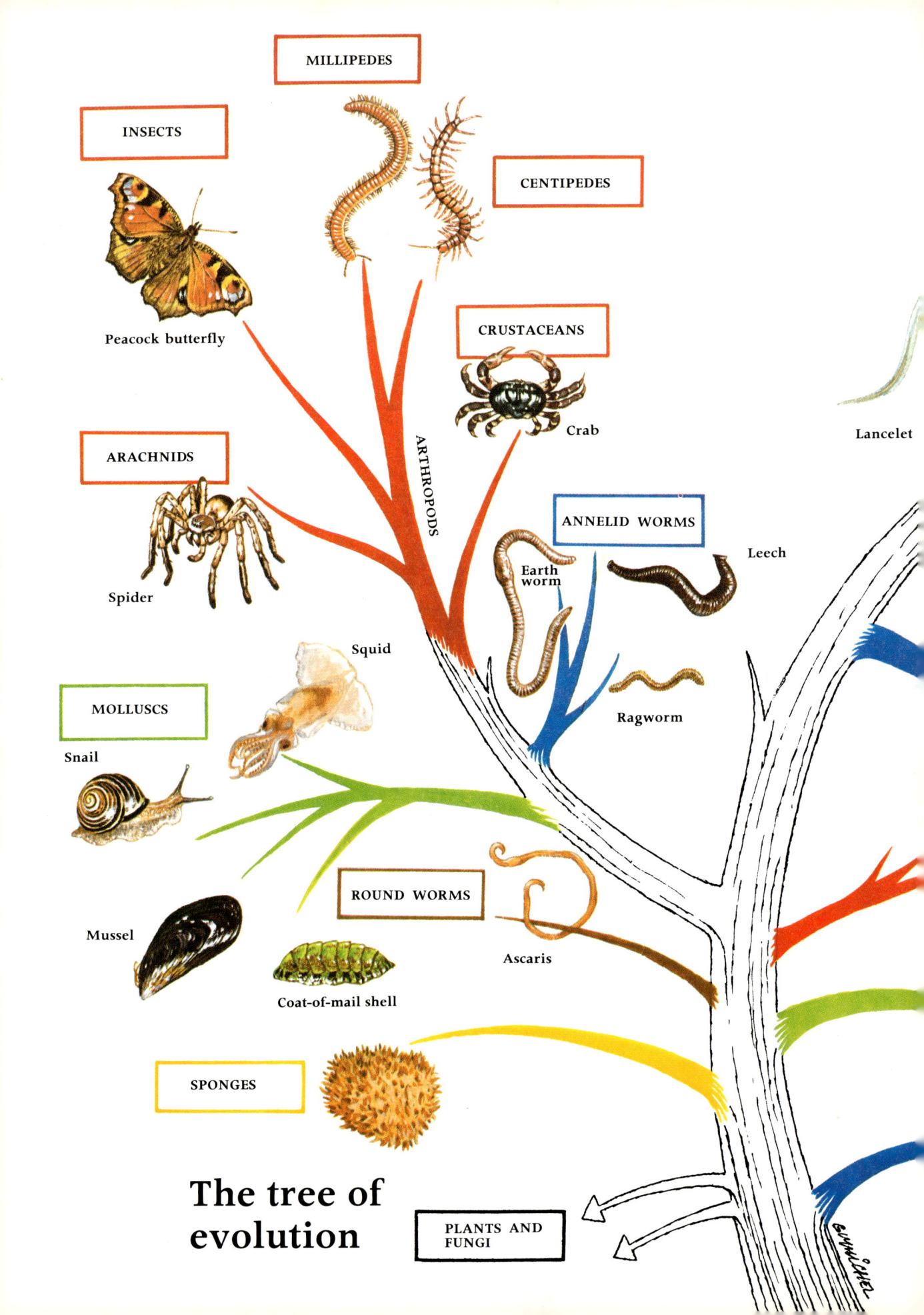

- MILLIPEDES
- INSECTS — Peacock butterfly
- CENTIPEDES
- CRUSTACEANS — Crab
- ARTHROPODS
- ARACHNIDS — Spider
- ANNELID WORMS — Earthworm, Leech, Ragworm
- Lancelet
- MOLLUSCS — Snail, Squid, Mussel, Coat-of-mail shell
- ROUND WORMS — Ascaris
- SPONGES
- PLANTS AND FUNGI

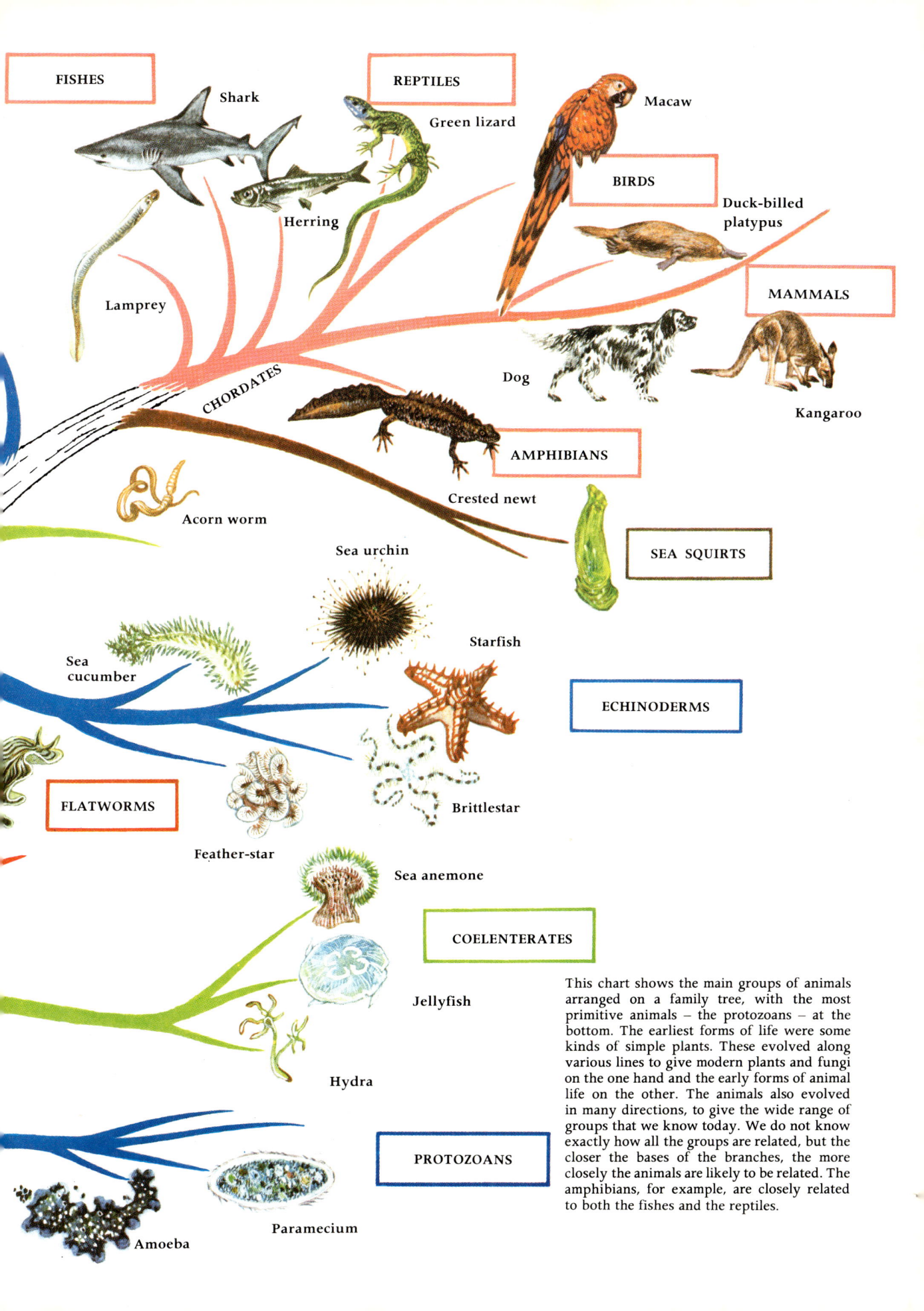

This chart shows the main groups of animals arranged on a family tree, with the most primitive animals – the protozoans – at the bottom. The earliest forms of life were some kinds of simple plants. These evolved along various lines to give modern plants and fungi on the one hand and the early forms of animal life on the other. The animals also evolved in many directions, to give the wide range of groups that we know today. We do not know exactly how all the groups are related, but the closer the bases of the branches, the more closely the animals are likely to be related. The amphibians, for example, are closely related to both the fishes and the reptiles.

INDEX

A
adder. See viper
albatross, 45
alligator snapper, 53
alligators, 50, 51
amoeba, 8, 88, 89, 91
amphibians, 58–9, 60, 91
anaconda, 56
angler fish, 65
animal kingdom,
    8–9 90–1
annelids, 86, 90
anteater, banded, 35
antelopes, 16, 17, 23, 24–5
ants, 79
apes, 18–19
apodans, 58
arachnids, 80, 81, 90
archer fish, 66
armadillos, 11
arthropods, 72, 80, 82, 91
ascaris, 90
asses, 16
axolotl, 59

B
baboon, 19
bacteria, 17
badger, 28–9
bandicoots, 34, 35
barnacles, 83
barracuda, 65
basking shark. See shark
bats, 10, 32, 33
bears, 26–7
    polar, 10, 26, 27
beaver, 20, 21
    lodge, 21
bees, 78–79
    nests, 28
beetles, 7, 76–7
    Goliath, 72
bell animalcule. See
    Vorticella
bird of paradise, 49
birds, 36–7, 91
    as food, 42
    flightless, 36, 38
    freshwater, 46–7
    hatching of, 37
    migration, 37
    wading, 45, 47
bison, 16
bitterling, 66
bittern, 47
bivalve, 68, 70, 84
blennies, 65
boa, 56
bony fish. See fish
booby, 45
bower birds, 49
brains, 10, 18

bristleworms, 86, 87
brittlestars, 84–5, 91
budgerigar, 40, 41
buffalo, 23
bugs, 73
butterflies, 72, 73, 74–5
    peacock, 90
buzzard, 36, 42

C
caddis fly,
    larvae, 73
caimans, 50
camels, 16
capybara, 20, 21, 66, 67
caracal, 22
carnivores, 9
carp, 66
carrion, 42
catfish, 67
cats, 22–23
cattle,
    domestic, 16
    use of grass, 17
centipedes, 72, 90
chaffinch, 36
chameleon, 54
cheetah, 22, 23
chelonians. See reptiles
chimpanzee, 18–19
chordates, 91
chrysalis, 75
coal-fish, 65
coat-of-mail shell, 90
cobra, 56, 57
cockatoo, 40, 41
cockle, 71, 84
cocoons, 75, 80
cod, 65
coelenterates, 85, 91
colobus, 19
colugo, 32
condor, 43
coral, 85
cormorant, 44
courtship displays, 49
cow, 10
cowrie, tiger, 71
coyote, 24
coypu, 21
crab, 72, 82–3, 90
    as a food source, 68, 69
cranefly, 76, 77
crayfish, 83
cricket, field, 73
crocodiles, 15, 50–1
crustaceans, 66, 82, 88, 90
    as a food source, 69
    marine, 82, 83
cuckoo, 37
curlew, 36, 37
cuttlefish, 68, 69
cyclostomes, 63

D
daddy-long-legs. See
    cranefly
deer, 16, 23, 24
    births, 11

red, 17
devil fish, 63
dinosaurs, descendants of,
    50
dodo, 36
dogs, 24–5, 91
dolphins, 30
dragonflies, 72, 73
ducks, 46
dugong, 31

E
eagles, 42, 43
earthworms, 86, 90
echinoderms, 84–5, 91
echo location, 32
eels, 62, 66, 67
elephants, 12–13
energy chain, 8
evolution, 9

F
falconet, 42
falcons, 42
    peregrine, 43
feather-star, 91
feathers,
    birds', 36, 38
fennec, 25
    See also fox
fireflies, 76
fish, 62–3, 64–5, 66–7, 91
    as a food, 42, 45, 51, 59
flamingos, 47
flatworms. See worms
flies, 72, 73, 76–7
food chain, 8, 31
foxes, 25
    births, 11
    flying. See bats
freshwater birds, 46–7
frigate bird, 45
frogs, 58, 60–1, 66
    as a food source, 51, 56,
        59
fungi, 90

G
gannets, 44
gastropods, 70
gavials, 50, 51
geckos, 55
geese, 46–7
gerbils, 20
gibbons, 19
gila monster, 54
giraffe, 9, 16
glow-worms, 73, 76
gnat. See mosquito
goats, 16, 17
goby, 65
    black, 63
gorilla, 18
grasshoppers, 73
grebes, 47
greenfly, 73, 76
guinea pig, 20
gulls, 45
    sea, 44

guppy, 67

H
haddock, 65
hagfishes, 63
hake, 65
hares, 10, 24
harriers, 42
harvestman, 81
hawkmoth, 74
hawks, 37, 42, 43
hedgehog, 11
heliozoan, 88
herbivores, 9
hermaphrodite, 71, 86
herons, 47
herring, 64, 91
hibernation, 32
hippopotamus, 14, 15
honey guide, 28
hoofs, 16–17
horns, 16
horses, 16
hummingbirds, 48, 49
hydra, 8, 85, 88, 89, 91

I
ichneumons, 73
iguana, 55
    marine, 54
insects, 72–9, 90
    as a food source, 42, 51,
        54, 56, 59, 60, 66, 81
invertebrates, 8, 68

J
jackal, 24
jaguar, 22
jellyfish, 85, 91
    as a food source, 52
jerboa, 21

K
kangaroos, 34, 35, 91
kea, 41
kestrel, 42
kingfisher, 37
kiwi, 36
koala, 34, 35
Komodo dragon, 54

L
ladybird, 76, 77
lampreys, 63, 66, 91
lancelet, 90–1
langurs, 19
leather-jacket, 77
leeches, 50, 86, 87, 90
lemmings, 21
lemurs,
    flying, 54
leopard, 22, 23
life processes, 89
ling, 65
lion, 10, 13, 22, 23
lizards, 50, 54–5, 91
    as a food source, 81
lobster, 82–3
lories, 41

lorikeets, 41
lugworm, 87
lungfish, 62
luth. See turtle, leathery
lynx, 23

M
macaws, 40, 41, 91
mackerel, 64
mallard,
  common, 46
mambas, 57
mammals, 10–11, 30–5, 91
  as a food source, 51
  hoofed, 16–17, 19
  in the air, 32–3
  in the sea, 30–1
  gnawing. See rodents
  with pouches, 34–5
mandrill, 19
man-o'-war bird. See
  frigate bird
marsupials, 34
martens, 29
matamata, 53
migration, 37
millipedes, 90
mink, 28
moles, 10, 34
molluscs, 66, 68, 70–1, 90
  as a food source, 84
monitors, 54
monkeys, 18–19
moorhen, 47
moose, 24
mosquito, 77, 88
mother-of-pearl, 70
moths, 72, 73, 74–5
mound-builders, 37
mountain lion. See puma
mouse, 20–1
  as a food source, 28
mouth brooder. See tilapia
mussels, 71, 90

N
nectar, 48, 74, 76, 78, 79
newts, 58, 91
  tadpoles, 61
numbat. See anteater,
  banded

O
ocelot, 23
octopus, 68–9
omnivores, 9
opossums, 34, 35
orang-utan, 18, 19
osprey, 42
ostrich, 36, 37
  eggs as food, 43
otters, 29
owls, 42, 43
oxpecker, 14
oyster, 71
oystercatcher, 45

P
panda, giant, 27

parakeets, 41
Paramecium, 88, 89, 91
parasites, 9, 86
parrots. 40–1
pearl, 70
pelicans, 47
penguins, 38–9
  as a food source, 31
phalangers, 32, 34, 35
pigs, 16
  as a food source, 57
pigeons, 36
pike, 66
pilchard, 64
piranhas, 66, 67
placenta, 11
plaice, 65
plankton, 65, 83
plants, 8, 90
platypus, duck-billed, 11, 91
pochard, 46
plover, Egyptian, 50
polecat, 28
pond skater, 73
porcupine fish, 65
porcupines, 20, 21
Portuguese man-o'-war, 85
praying mantis, 73
prawns, 65, 83
  as a food source, 69
primates, 18
proboscis, 74
pronghorn antelope, 16
protozoans, 8, 88, 89, 91
puffin, 47
puma, 23
pupae, 75
puss moth, 75
pythons, 56, 57

Q
queen substance, 78

R
rabbit, 10, 11
rabies, 33
radiolarian, 88
radula, 70, 71
ratel. See badger, honey
rats, 20
  as a food source, 42
rattlesnakes, 57
rays, 63, 65
razorshell, 71
redshank, 45
reindeer, 16, 24
reptiles, 50–1, 56–7, 91
  descendants of, 36
  with shells, 52–3
rhinoceroses, 14–15, 16
rodents, 20–1, 24
  as a food source, 42
  number in births, 11
  teeth, 20

S
sable, 28
saithe, 65

salamanders, 58, 59, 61
salmon, 66, 67
sandpipers, 45
scallop, 71
scorpions, 80–1
  as a food source, 19
sea anemone, 8, 71, 84–5, 91
sea birds, 65
sea cows, 30
sea cucumber, 85, 91
sea-gulls. See gulls
sea hare, 70–71
seahorse, 64, 65
sea lily, 8, 85
sea lions, 31
seals, 30, 31, 38
  as a food source, 31
sea squirts, 91
sea urchin, 84–5, 91
secretary bird, 9, 42
serpula, 87
serval, 23
sharks, 63, 65, 91
sheep, 16, 41
shrimps, 83
  as a food source, 68, 69, 85
silkworm, 75
skates, 63, 65
skink, 55
skuas, 39
skunk, 29
sleeping platforms, 18, 19
slow-worm, 55
slugs, 68, 70–1
  as a food source, 59, 60
snails, 68, 70–1, 90
snakes, 50, 56–7
  as a food source, 42
  skin-shedding, 56
sole, 65
sow bug. See woodlice
sparrowhawk, 42
sparrows, 36
spiders, 72, 80–1, 88, 90
spirographis. See
  bristleworm
sponges, 90
sprats, 64
squid, 45, 65, 68, 69, 90
  as a food source, 31, 38
squirrels, 20
  flying, 32, 35
starfish, 8, 84–5, 91
stentor, 88
stick insect, 72
stickleback, 66, 67
stoat, 28
swallows, 36, 37
swans, 46–7

T
tadpoles, 58, 61
tail, prehensile, 19, 35
tapeworm, 86
tapirs, 16
tarantula. See spider
Tasmanian devil, 35

tellin, 71
tench, 66, 67
termites, 79
  as a food source, 27, 35
terrapins, 52
tiger moth, 75
tigers, 13, 22, 23
tilapia, 67
tits,
  long-tailed, 37
toads, 58, 60–1
tortoises, 52–3
tortoiseshell, 53
toucan, 48
trout, 66
tunny, 64, 65, 69
turtles, 50, 52–3

U
ungulates. Also mammals,
  hoofed
  even-toed, 16
  odd-toed 16
urchins, 84

V
venom, snake, 57
vertebrates, 8
vipers, 56, 57
voles,
  as a food source, 28
Vorticella, 88
vultures, 42, 43

W
wading birds, 45
wallabies, 34
walrus, 31
warble-fly, 77
warblers, 36
wasps, 78–9
water flea, 83, 88, 89
water mites, 88
weasels, 28
weevil, grain, 76
whale shark, 63
whales, 8, 10, 30, 31, 63
  births, 11
whiting, 65
wildcat, European, 23
wildebeest, 23
wolf, 24–5
  prairie. See coyote
  Tasmanian, 34
wolverine, 29
wombats, 34, 35
woodlice, 83
woodpeckers, 36, 37
woodworm. See beetles
worms, 86–7, 90
  acorn, 91
  as a food source, 44, 65, 66
  flat, 86, 87, 91
  ragworm, 90
  round, 86, 90

Z
zebra, 10, 16, 17, 23